REFUGEE STORIES

In Their Own Words

Laurie Nowell

Published by:
Wilkinson Publishing Pty Ltd
ACN 006 042 173
Level 4, 2 Collins Street
Melbourne, Vic 3000
Ph: 03 9654 5446
www.wilkinsonpublishing.com.au

 A catalogue record for this book is available from the National Library of Australia

Planned date of publication: 10-2018
Title: Refugee Stories, in their own words
ISBN(s): 9781925642735: Printed - Paperback

Design by Spike Creative Pty Ltd
Ph: (03) 9427 9500
spikecreative.com.au

Printed in Australia by Ligare

'In this book there are leading doctors, artists and musicians; there are people building successful small businesses; there are people simply relishing life in a safe and hospitable new home. The common thread is that they have all escaped from different but all unimaginable horrors and dangers, and have undertaken perilous journeys to reach the safe haven that Australia offers refugees. This book reminds us that the sometimes-strident rhetoric around refugees in Australia hides the real people who have lived through more pain and terror than we can comprehend; and who can, do and will continue to make wonderful contributions to our society — as refugees have done throughout our country's recent history.'

Stuart Crosby, *AMES Australia Chair*

'This book is timely reminder of the resilience, courage and optimism that refugees have always brought to this country. It was people just like those described in these pages who have helped shaped this country over many decades.'

Peter Scanlon, *Chair Scanlon Foundation*

'These stories about fleeing war torn countries and escaping from persecution are really stories of survival, courage and determination. In accepting and supporting the people behind these stories, the generosity and humanity of Australia shines ever so bright. But the benefit is not all one way. Years later, these stories continue and evolve on our shores. A leading medical expert, a national poetry winner, a mayor, business owners and other trail blazers. All contributing to the dynamism and growth of Australia.'

Huy Truong, *CEO Aligroup*

CONTENTS

FOREWORD

PROTECTING REFUGEES IS A RESPONSIBILITY AND A PRIVILEGE

We believe refugees make a unique contribution to Australia and it is important to share the incredible stories that stem from the largest human displacement crisis in history.

Each year Australia takes in about 18,000 refugees. Since our humanitarian program commenced shortly after World War II, it has offered sanctuary to almost a million people. From Europeans escaping the ravages of a global conflict through to the Vietnamese in the 1970s, Croatians and Bosnians in the 1990s and, more recently, people from Africa and the Middle East, Australia has provided a new life for generations of displaced people.

Among these arrivals were many great entrepreneurs and people who made significant contributions but also, importantly, there were people like you and me — working hard to establish safe and secure futures for our children.

In recent times many of the people who have arrived here have come from Syria or Iraq as victims of the brutal conflict still raging there. We took an extra 12,000 people fleeing this conflict because then prime minister Tony Abbott saw that the need for resettlement places far outstripped the number available.

Australia has a very generous and sophisticated refugee settlement program that is among the highest per-capita intakes of any country in the world. The program provides support for refugees to integrate and become economically independent and socially connected — which is one reason why we have high social cohesion in this country.

The reason refugees come to Australia is not primarily to work and contribute to our economy — although they do — or to speak English and integrate with the rest of us — which they also largely do — it is because they need protection. For them to remain in their homelands means being subjected violence, persecution or worse. Many refugees who have found their way to Australia have suffered torture or trauma, some have lost everything they owned or held dear and others have lost family members.

Australia was one of the earliest signatories to the 1951 United Nations Convention on Refugees. The convention stemmed from WWII and the Holocaust and it was designed so that we would never again see people at grave risk of death or persecution turned away by countries where they sought sanctuary. The convention lays out and binds signatory countries to the legal notion of 'non-refoulement' — which means that a nation cannot forcibly return someone to a country where they are likely to be subjected to persecution.

Among the thousands of desperate people supported by my organisation AMES Australia was an Iranian forensic scientist whom we will call 'Nik'. His story is published in this book. Nik, an ethnic Arab, was tortured and jailed for refusing to produce bogus drug reports on anti-government dissidents in Iran. Drugs offences in Iran usually carry the death penalty so for refusing to effectively condemn to death people opposed to the government of Iran, Nik himself was subjected to torture and the threat of death. On his release, he escaped from Iran and sought refuge in Australia.

Another story published in this book is that of a young Afghan man named Amini, who was a bookbinder in his home town of Kabul. When he published a copy of the Koran in the local Dari language an extremist cleric issued a fatwah (death sentence) on Amini. He was forced into hiding as gangs of extremist militia searched for him. He left Afghanistan as soon he could and sought sanctuary in Australia.

The reason these two men, and thousands more like them, are in Australia is not because they speak English and can contribute to our economy, nor is it because they will 'fit in'. It is simply because they had no other option.

We all need to remember that the world is embroiled in the worst refugee crisis in history with 68 million people displaced from their homes. Refugees are here because normal life in their home countries is untenable and they need protection. We need to continue to support and protect our refugee program and promote it to the world. If other western nations made available as many permanent resettlement places per capita as Australia does, it would mean that each year hundreds of thousands more of the world's most vulnerable people could find a safe place to live.

Cath Scarth CEO, AMES Australia

INTRODUCTION

The global refugee crisis has been called one of the great moral challenges of our time and if all of the displaced people in the world were a single nation, it would be larger than Britain or France. The number of people fleeing conflicts across the globe has soared to more than 68 million — about one per cent of the world's total population — and the highest level ever recorded. That figure is up from 65.3 million in 2016 and 59.5 million in 2015, and amounts to 20 people being displaced every minute of the day. Most of these people have fled conflicts in Syria, Afghanistan, South Sudan, Myanmar and Somalia. Most have found temporary refuge in countries like Turkey, Pakistan, Uganda and Lebanon; nations that largely struggle to support the great numbers of people seeking safety. Eighty-five per cent of the world's refugees are hosted in developing nations.

According to the United Nations, there are about 25 million people deemed to be refugees, 40 million internally displaced people and three million asylum seekers. There are also 1.2 million people in urgent need of resettlement. The number of resettlement places reached a 20-year high of 120,000 in 2016. Since then that has decreased, with just 75,000 places available in 2018. So, 90 per cent of those in need of resettlement will never have the opportunity to make a new life somewhere else and will likely live out a large proportion of their lives in camps.

Underpinning the refugee crisis is global socio-political turmoil and local polarised politics that has demonised refugees and, fuelled by a notion that globalisation has brought inequality and instability, made the futures of displaced people more precarious than at any other time in modern history.

Australia is one of just 35 countries that welcome refugees permanently under the United Nations High Commission for Refugees (UNHCR) program. The nation accepts around 18,000 refugees each year. By contrast, last year Japan accepted just 28.

Notwithstanding criticism of the way the nation treats asylum seekers, and especially those in offshore detention, Australia has one of the most generous and sophisticated refugee resettlement programs, taking in one refugee for every 1,400 Australians each year. Since World War II, Australia has accepted 800,000 refugees from all over the planet. And about a third of those have settled in Melbourne.

Melbourne and Sydney especially have become a beacon to some refugee communities. For Afghan Hazaras living in limbo and without official status in Pakistan or Iran, Dandenong, in Melbourne's south east, is almost a promised land. And for Burmese Karen refugees living in camps on the Thai border, Werribee, in Melbourne's west is a place where many of the countrymen have built new lives. In Sydney, Auburn and Cabramatta have seen the settlement of large numbers of people from the Middle-East and Indo-China respectively.

A recent study shows that Australia's refugee arrivals between 2010 and 2017 were predominantly from Afghanistan, Iraq, Syria, Burma/ Myanmar and Iran. Between 2001 and 2011 they came mostly from Sudan, Iraq, Afghanistan and Burma/Myanmar and refugees formed 12 per cent of all arrivals to Victoria in 2011. In Melbourne, large populations of refugees live in the local government areas of Greater Dandenong, Hume, Casey, Brimbank and Wyndham and each area has people from a diverse range of countries with associated language needs. In Sydney, the cities of Fairfield and Auburn are host to large numbers of refugees. Refugee groups are attracted to areas with affordable housing with about two-thirds of refugee arrivals in Victoria in 2011 living in the 20 per cent most socio-disadvantaged areas in the state.

The other thing we know about refuges is that they are keen to fit in and contribute. Australia Bureau of Statistics data shows overwhelmingly that refugees and migrants are embracing life in Australia while attempting to adopt the nation's culture and traditions. The snapshot of permanent migrants who have arrived in Australia this century reveals most of them work, are buying or own a home, have acquired high-level English language skills and become citizens. The data, which looks at permanent migrants who arrived in Australia between 1 January 2000, and 9 August 2016 shows almost 60 per cent of migrants and one third of humanitarian refugees owned or were buying a house. It reveals that 64 per cent of migrants and 78 per cent of refugees had become Australian citizens. But as writer Paul Brodeur said, 'statistics are human beings with the tears wiped away'.

The refugees who settle in Australia bring with them memories, traditions, culture and history. They also bring with them hopes, dreams and ambitions for their children. They are, by definition, resilient and ingenious people who have overcome challenges and dangers just to get here.

This book is about the experiences and the hopes and dreams of refugees who have settled in Australia and also about those in our society who have tried to make them feel welcome. These are inspirational stories of ordinary people forced by circumstances beyond their control to make extraordinary physical and emotional journeys to safety and freedom.

CHAPTER I
SURVIVING ISIS – A REFUGEE'S STORY

Syrian refugee George (not his real name) survived a year as a captive of ISIS, treated brutally, constantly threatened with death and not knowing the fate of his wife and daughter. Now safe and living in Melbourne's north, George has shared the details of his incredible ordeal in the hope that the international community increases its efforts to help the millions of refugees who have not found a safe place to rebuild their lives.

'I was fortunate to survive and to find a safe place to live with my family. But there are many, many people who are still in very difficult circumstances even though the threat of ISIS has gone,' he said.

George shared his story through an interpreter on the proviso that his identity and details about his life not be revealed to protect the lives of family members still in Syria.

A professional, who studied at Damascus University and then in Europe and returned to Syria in 1995, George is from a small village of 400 people about 30 kilometres from the city of Al Hasakah in northern Syria. It is one of 33 small Assyrian Christian villages along the Khabur River, close to the Turkish border, that were once home to about 20,000 people. George said that as the conflict in Syria escalated in 2014 the security situation in his area began to deteriorate.

Even listening to George through an interpreter, his understated, sometimes humourous tone betrays a quiet courage and gentle humility. 'Sometimes I could get to work, sometimes I couldn't,' he said. 'We knew things were getting worse when the army started to withdraw from the Al Hasakah suburbs.'

Then, early on the morning of 23 February 2015, ISIS attacked the villages. Heavily armed ISIS fighters stormed his village just after 8am.

'There were 200 of us captured by ISIS including all of my family members. They put us in a house in the middle of the village and started to threaten us with guns and shout at us,' George said. 'They said to us, "you are kafir (unbelievers) and this is not your land…", they asked us who gave us permission to build churches. We stayed for six hours in this house. We were full of fear and we didn't know if they were going to kill us. Every moment we thought, maybe they will kill us now.'

The villagers were put into trucks and the ISIS fighters tried to take them to a mountain base 30 kilometres away but the column was attacked by Kurdish militia and forced to retreat back to the village.

After spending a night crammed in the house and having to sleep standing, the group was finally transferred to Mt Abdul Aziz, a fortified ridge controlled by ISIS. 'At this point we — the men — were separated from the women and children. This was the worst moment for us we didn't know what would happen to our women and children,' George said.

The men were put in closed trucks and taken to the town of Al Shadada. 'We couldn't see anything, we could hardly breathe and there were shots being fired around us,' George said. 'When we arrived at the town, we were put in a prison and the ISIS men took everything we had — ID, money, everything. And they started asking us about our names. At that moment we didn't know what was happening or whether we were going to die or not.'

The men were placed in a house under guard — thirty people to a room. 'When I got to the house I was surprised to see people from other villages there too. There were around 300-350 of us,' George said. But we still didn't know what had happened to our women and kids and didn't see them for three months.'

George said that Muslim clerics told the men that they must convert to Islam or they would be killed.

The joy of finally being able to see their children after three months was tempered when they learned that one 15-year-old girl had been taken away and 'given' to the local ISIS Sheikh. 'To this day we do not know what happened to this girl. I knew the girl and her family because they lived in a nearby village. When we saw our kids they did not recognise us because we had been forced to grow long beards. When they saw us they asked, "are you ISIS?".'

George concluded that he and the other Christians were being used as a bargaining chip. 'We knew they had killed a lot of people so during this time we didn't know what they wanted from us. They said they wanted something and if they didn't get it they would kill us,' he said. 'Every day we grew more fearful that we would die. And we thought that if ISIS didn't kill us we would die from the shelling and bombing that was going on overhead.'

He said that as time went by the conditions under which the men were being held worsened. 'There were 150 of us in one small house with one bathroom and one toilet,' George said. 'We were given a little food — just bread and vegetables we had to cook'.

George said he began to recognise the accents of his ISIS guards and was surprised to discover the international nature of the group. 'There were Tunisians, French, and Saudi Arabians. The local Prince was an Iraqi,' he said. 'We were all very scared of these men. They looked scary and they were fanatics. They told us they believed that each time they killed a Christian, they would get to paradise.'

George said that in the fourth month of their captivity the men were moved to a house closer to the front lines. 'It was a very dangerous area. Above our apartment we could hear voices and many different languages,' he said. 'There was shelling and shooting and aircraft going over all of the time. It felt like they were shooting at us. We heard explosions but we didn't know what was going on. After 20 days in this place a group of people — a committee — came to ask questions about who we were, what we thought about the government — if we were with or against the government — if we knew our destiny. They said that Sharia law said that our destiny was Islam or death. We told them we were peaceful, not with or against anyone and that we were not armed.'

At this point the men were given an ultimatum to convert to Islam or die.

'We never discussed it as a group but each man said that he would rather die than convert to Islam,' George said. 'This was the worst moment. After the committee talked to us, a group of armed men came in led by a Tunisian who told us to get ready to die. He insulted us and swore at our religion. Then we were taken one by one to another room where they searched us and threatened us.'

George said the worst moment of his captivity came when ISIS picked six single men and took them away. Three of the men, Bassam, Ashour and Abdalmasaya — all of them his friends — never returned.

'Bassam and Ashour were very kind people who helped the older men in our group. Some of the group were paralysed and they helped feed and bathe them,' George said. 'Abdalmasaya was a doctor who used to treat and help people who got sick in our group. He was the most optimistic of us and he was always telling people we would be set free soon.'

George said the three men were shot and killed on Eid night.

'We learned later they were made to wear orange jumpsuits and taken out in a car and driven for an hour,' he said. 'ISIS told them not to worry, that they were just filming a frightening video and were not going to kill them. This is what ISIS tell people to keep them calm. But they shot our friends. However, Ashour didn't die immediately so they put them in a grave and shot him again. The three others were made to watch this happen and they were told they would be next if they didn't obey their captors.'

After this incident, the men were moved to Raqqa and it was here, after six months, that they gained the first inkling as to what had happened to their families. ISIS were shuffling prisoners around buildings in Raqqa as the areas they controlled shrank in the face of advances by the Syrian army and militia groups.

George said the women and children had been held in a part of the prison that the men later occupied. 'Some of the women left behind signs that they had been there. It was very clever of them. We could tell they had been there because they left personal items that some of the men recognised. We knew they were safe and we were very relieved to know they were still alive,' he said.

As the fighting closed in around Raqqa, the threat of death at the hands of ISIS or as a result of shelling loomed larger.

'The building the prison was in was shelled many times and we feared that if ISIS didn't kill us the shelling would,' George said. 'At this time, we could hear ISIS torturing people somewhere in the prison. There were screams — usually after midnight. They didn't torture us and after three or four months they said they would set some of us free but we didn't know if they were lying to us. But then they started setting groups of people free and my turn came in January 2016. I was among the last.'

After 11 months in captivity, living constantly with the threat of death and fearful for the fate of his family, George regained his freedom.

'They blindfolded us and put us in a van. At the time we didn't know what had happened to the people set free before us so we thought we were going to be killed,' George said. 'But when we got to this place, there was a bus waiting for us. We were five men, seven women and some children and we were free.'

George learned his wife and daughter had been set free 20 days earlier. He was taken to the town of Tall Tamer and reunited with his family. He has never returned to his village. He and his family spent a month in Tall Tamer living with cousins. When he managed to obtain a new passport, the family left for Lebanon.

After six months in Lebanon, the family was granted a humanitarian visa by the Australian embassy in Beirut and they arrived in Melbourne in December 2016.

George says that no one among his fellow captives has returned to their village but that the bonds formed during their desperate times remain strong even though the group is now spread across the globe.

'My personal story is also a group story,' he said. 'I got close to my fellow captives. We used to help each other. For example, the young people encouraged the older ones, telling them not to worry, and the older people gave us advice and wisdom.'

He said that it was his wish to see his daughter grow up that kept him alive through the ordeal.

'If you put someone even in a hotel for a couple of months, they'll go crazy. What kept me sane in captivity was the thought that I had to live for my daughter,' George said.

And he said that he always harboured a sense of destiny about his survival. He is the third generation of his family to have had to flee their homes. 'My grandfather fled from Turkey to Iraq during the Armenian genocide in 1918 and my father fled the Simele massacre in Iraq in 1933. So, I always knew our family is a family of survivors,' George said.

Safe in Melbourne, George is now looking to the future. He hopes to resume his career and says his daughter is doing well in school. 'We are grateful to be here and to have safety. It is a good life in Australia and my daughter is very happy in her school. We hope for a better future for her,' he said.

And asked about his captors and killers of his friends, he says he forgives them. 'I can't hate anyone. I took the quote from my friend Abdalmasaya. He wrote a note to his killer — as Jesus Christ did — saying "I forgive you".'

CHAPTER 2
STORIES OF THE ROHINGYA

Members of Australia's refugee Rohingya community have shared their personal stories in in a bid to highlight the plight of their compatriots, who after becoming the victims of a bloody and ruthless crackdown by the Burmese military, are now languishing in refugee camps in Bangladesh.

'We want to the Australian people to know what's happening to the Rohingya and that the Burmese Government is lying to the world,' said Rohingya community leader Abdul Hamid.

The number of Rohingya refugees who have fled the violence in Myanmar has now hit a staggering 950,000 just a year after exodus began.

MAJID ABDUL

A simple Google search convinced Burmese Rohingya refugee Majid that Australia was the only place he could build a new life; free from the persecution and the threat of prison or death in his homeland and the penurious hand-to-mouth existence he had fallen into in Malaysia and Indonesia.

Now in Australia, Majid has rebuilt his life but he fears for the hundreds of thousands of Rohingya still in Burma or in refugee camps in neighbouring Bangladesh.

Majid was a student in Burma but only because his parents had enough money to bribe the authorities to let him enrol in school. Generally, in Burma Rohingya are not allowed to study beyond primary school. Majid finished primary school in his village and went on to the high school and then higher education. He had to leave his village to take on higher education but being away from his family and his precarious status as a Rohingya took its toll.

'There was a lot of discrimination against us and I was beaten up by my classmates,' Majid said. 'In the end I felt it was not worthwhile and

I knew there would be no job for me after I finished. I was abused at school when we played soccer, the other boys would kick me instead of the ball because I was Rohingya. I wore pants to school but I was told I was not allowed to because my people traditionally wore sarongs. I wanted just peace and to be left alone at school that didn't happen.'

Majid moved to the capital Yangon hoping things would be better. He stayed with relatives there but was forced to flee again.

'The police would come to your house at midnight asking to see peoples ID cards. I didn't have one so I was scared,' he said. 'Eventually my relatives didn't want me because if I had been arrested it would have been a big problem for them. Finally, I decided to flee to Thailand and I walked across the border and from there went to Malaysia. There are some Rohingya in Malaysia and I thought I could find some work there.'

He found work in construction but was paid paltry wages and sometimes none at all. 'I had to work to survive but I was not paid very much and sometimes they didn't pay me at all,' Majid said. 'The police arrested me many times. I had no documents and I tried to explain that I was Rohingya and the Burmese government didn't give me any ID. I told them that if they sent me back, the Burmese government would kill me. Each time I bribed them and they released me.'

Majid said he realised he needed to find somewhere new where he could build a new life.

'We were not of value to anyone in Malaysia. The police would often take our money because they could,' he said. 'And I was worried about my parents and how they would feel if I was sent back and killed by the government. I did some research using Google and I came up with Australia as the best country for me and I decided I would try to get here. We knew it was risky to go by boat to Australia but we decided it was better to die at sea than to go on living the way we were.'

Majid worked and saved money and eventually crossed the border into Indonesia among a group of eight Rohingya. He said the group couldn't find any smugglers to take them so they pooled resources and bought and old fishing boat. Not knowing anything about boats or navigation, they hired an Indonesian crew.

'We didn't really know where we were going and after five days and five nights we were still in Indonesia. We thought we were in Australia but we were arrested and sent to a detention camp at Kupang,' Majid said.

He said the group was interviewed by the UN but were not accepted as refugees because they had no identification. 'We were sent from Kupang to Medan, also in a detention camp, but the UNHCR gave us some better accommodation there,' he said. 'I asked them how long we would be there and they said some people had been there ten years. It was then that I realised that I had to get myself to Australia.'

Majid joined another group and they bought another boat and after four days they arrived at Christmas Island.

'This was in 2009. I spent five months on Christmas Island and then was transferred to Darwin. I had finally made it to Australia,' he said.

Majid spent a total of two years in detention in Australia before being released in 2011. He now lives and works in Melbourne and has applied for Australian citizenship. But that has been held up because he does not have identity documents.

'I have started a new life here. I'm safe and this is where I will stay,' he said.

Recently Majid, who now works in the community sector, recently bought his first house in Melbourne's south east.

ABDUL HAMID

Burmese Rohingya refugee Abdul Hamid spent four years doing hard labour in prison for simply leaving his village. He had been trying to visit relatives in Sittwe, the capital of Burma's Rakhine state, when he was arrested by the police.

'I was going to visit some relatives in the city and the police stopped me and arrested me. I was taken to Yangon and I went to court,' Abdul said. I tried to explain I was going to Sittwe to see my family but they didn't listen to me. I was jailed for four years and I never found out what I was charged with.'

Abdul said jail in Burma was a traumatic experience. 'It was horrible and very dangerous. And you had to work to eat,' he said. 'My family didn't know where I was. They thought I was dead. After two years a person from the IOM (International Organisation for Migration) visited the prison and wrote a letter to my family telling them where I was. There were 200 people in my cell and there was not a proper place to sleep. We had to guard each other at night so we wouldn't be attacked and robbed of what little we had. I worked making bricks in jail and we had to grow our own food to eat. We were told the prison had no budget to feed us so we had to work — but there was never enough food.'

Abdul said there were about 1,000 Rohingya in prison with him in Yangon. He was released after four years and decided immediately to leave the country. Abdul travelled to Thailand and then Malaysia and Indonesia. He was married in Malaysia in 2010 and his first child was born in 2011. The following year, with their one-year-old son in their arms, Abdul and his wife made the perilous boat journey to Christmas Island.

'We arrived there on April 1, my child's first birthday,' Abdul said. 'All my life in Burma I was persecuted by the Burmese authorities and the Burmese people. I was not allowed to go to school. I was stopped many times by the police on my way to school and told I was not a citizen and so I was not allowed to go to school. One day, I remember, I was going school and a couple of Buddhist people stopped me, abused me and beat me. I could never have gotten a job in Burma — we had no right to work — and my family always faced discrimination. Now, I have a good life in Australia but I worry about my family still in Burma.'

Abdul works in gardening and landscaping in Melbourne's south east.

ARIFULLAH

Fears that the police would come to his village and kill him convinced Burmese Rohingya refugee Arifullah that he had no future in his homeland.

'Life was very difficult for us. We could not study, we had no work and really no life,' Arifullah said. 'When the political situation got worse we were scared of the local police. People were killed or just disappeared. They were particularly targeting young men so I decided I needed to get out.'

He came to Australia by boat in 2013 and is now on a bridging visa and studying project management. But he has grave fears for his family who have fled to Bangladesh in the wake of the Burmese military's bloody and ruthless crackdown on the Rohingya people.

'Life for my family in Bangladesh is very difficult. They are living in crowded and dangerous places,' Arifullah said. 'There is fever and sickness there and we trying to do everything we can to help them.'

CHAPTER 3
WELCOME TO CARLTON: SYRIAN FAMILY THE LATEST CHAPTER IN AN ENDURING MIGRANT STORY

Akram Abouhamdan and his wife Joumana have just opened the first Syrian food shop on Lygon Street, in the historic Melbourne suburb of Carlton. The shop — which sells Syrian sweets and dips, baklava and handmade pasta — is quietly symbolic. Nestled among the Italian eateries along the famous strip, it represents the latest wave of migration to arrive in Melbourne. It also represents the hopes and dreams of a refugee family who have had to flee their home, their lives and everything they once held dear in their homeland Syria.

But Akram and Joumana's story is slightly different from most people fleeing the five-year-long conflict in Syria. They did not flee because their home was destroyed or because of fighting in their neighbourhood. They left because they were persecuted and threatened for supporting others left helpless by the war.

A successful businessman and a lawyer by training, Akram ran a successful food distribution business in the southern city of As-Suwayda, which has remained relatively untouched by the brutal conflict that has engulfed much of the country.

And even as members of the minority Druze faith, he and his family had no particular argument with the government of Syria or its president Bashar al-Assad.

That all changed for the Abouhamdans when refugees from other parts of Syria started flooding into their city.

'There were so many people who had fled the fighting and had literally nothing, we had to do something to help them,' Akram said.

Akram, with the help of two brothers working overseas as well as other family and friends, set up a reception centre to house and feed women and children who had fled the brutal conflict elsewhere in Syria.

'When the uprising began and fighting started in 2012 refugees began to come to our city,' Akram said. 'We made a place where they could stay and be safe and we provided food and blankets. We were accommodating 2,500 people.'

But because most of the people being sheltered by the Abouhamdans came from areas where militia groups were opposing the Assad regime, the government considered them the wives and children of 'terrorists'.

'To us they were just people in need who posed no threat to anyone so we felt we had to help them,' Akram said. 'The government didn't like what we were doing so I was called in by the security police for an interview, They said "you have to stop helping these terrorists" even though they were all women and children. But we didn't stop. We had 2,500 people who were depending on us.'

Akram began hiding from the security services. Several times they arrived at his home to arrest him but he stayed with friends and moved frequently.

Akram told how one of his friends who helped out at the shelter was arrested and held for seven months. 'They tortured him and drilled holes in his legs. He is still having treatment for that and struggles to walk,' he said. 'If they had caught me they would have killed me. I would have just disappeared.'

Eventually Akram was forced to flee to Jordan leaving his family behind. He had earlier sent his son to safety in Lebanon.

'I had to leave Syria, the shelter closed down and I do not know what happened to the people who were living there. I still worry about that,' Akram said.

After a desperate time in the Zaatari refugee camp, infamous for food shortages and crime gangs, Akram moved to stay with friends in the city of Irbid where Joumana and his younger son and daughter joined him.

The family came to Australia as refugees in November 2014. 'We are grateful to have found safety here in Australia. The people here are very good, very friendly and everyone wants to help you,' Akram said.

As Akram says this, the man who runs the café next door stops by to smile and say hello.

But things have not been easy for the family. Akram has struggled to find work and his son is having difficulty securing a place at a college or university to be able to continue his studies in architecture. 'We feel very safe in Australia but it's not easy to change your life; to have a new language and a new culture,' Akram said. 'But we had to do something to support ourselves and my wife is a very good cook. So, we made baklava and Syrian sweets and started selling them from a stall at the markets.'

Joumana had been working with the social enterprise SisterWorks, which supports women of migrant, asylum seeker or refugee backgrounds to develop handmade food or craft products in order to become financially independent. For two years the family sold their delicious wares at markets around Melbourne while also learning English with refugee and migrant settlement agency AMES Australia. Then they took a leap of faith and leased a shop in Carlton, following in the footsteps of migrants and refugees down the decades.

'So far things are going well. Life in Australia is good for us. We are safe here and we are grateful to Australia,' he said.

The shop, called 'Trio', is at 339 Lygon Street, Carlton.

CHAPTER 4
FINDING FAMILY – A REFUGEE'S JOURNEY BACK

As a young child Hamdi Ubeed was taken from her family by an 'aunt' who promised to remove her from the dangers of the then raging Somalian civil war. The 'aunt' — a distant relative of her father — and her extended family escaped the brutal conflict, but along the way Hamdi's name was changed and all trace of her biological family wiped away. And instead of safety, peace and a new life, what followed for Hamdi were years of fear, heartache and betrayal.

'My aunt asked my family if she could take me to a better place so she adopted me and we moved to a camp in Egypt,' Hamdi said. 'My aunt changed my last name, she counted me as one of her kids and she told everyone I was her daughter.'

After years as refugees in camps in Egypt the family was eventually granted resettlement places in Australia in 2000.

When she turned 15 in 2006, Hamdi found out she had been adopted and announced that she wanted to find her biological family. Her 'aunt' immediately threw her out of their home.

'I found out my "aunt" wasn't my real mum when I heard the other kids talking,' Hamdi said. 'I told her "I need to look for my family and my mum and dad". My aunt said if I did, she would throw me out. I decided I had to know what had happened to my family, so she threw me out of the house. She said "I don't care where you go. Just go".'

Hamdi was taken in by a cousin and she began improving her English attending a language school in Melbourne's west. But one day she became lost after getting on the wrong bus. 'I could not speak much English and I did not know where I was. I couldn't ask anyone for help,' Hamdi said. 'I was very scared, I didn't know what to do.'

Eventually she was approached by a Somali taxi driver who took her to some members of the Somali community in Footscray and eventually her cousin was tracked down and she was taken home. It was these accidental community connections that eventually connected her with her biological family after a four-year search.

She met a Somali man who frequently travelled to East Africa for business. 'I asked him if he could ask about my family and eventually he got word that my family was living in a small town in western Somalia called Abudwak,' Hamdi said.

In 2011, at just 20-years-of-age, Hamdi travelled alone to her homeland to find her family. After a flight to Abu Dhabi, two internal flights in Somalia and a 16-hour mini-bus ride, she found her family. 'It was very emotional and wonderful to meet my family after so long. They were very surprised, they didn't know I was coming,' Hamdi said. 'My family knew I was overseas somewhere but not where. And because my name had been changed, they had no way of finding me. At first, I was taken to my uncle's house and then he took me to see my mum and brothers. She was crying and I was crying.'

She spent three happy months living with her family in Abudwak before returning to Australia. But tragedy seems never far away in her blighted homeland. Soon after she left, a savage drought struck the area where her family was living and they were forced to move to the capital Mogadishu. At the time the Islamic militant group Al Shabaab controlled vast swathes of the city and they came to Hamdi's mother's house and kidnapped two of her brothers.

'Some men came to my mother's house and kidnapped two of my brothers. They were from Al Shabaab — this is a group that is very bad, they take teenagers and brainwash them and make them fight for them,' Hamdi said. 'At the time my mother was at home with my brothers and she refused to let them go but the men hit my mother with the butt of their guns and they took my brothers with them. We don't know what happened to them and we have never heard from them again.'

Fearing for her other three sons, Hamdi's mother fled to Kenya where they spent six months in the Dadaab refugee camp — the world's largest.

But violence and threats there forced her to flee again in 2012 — this time to the only slightly smaller Kakuma camp, where they remain.

Now 26 and married, Hamdi works in a child care centre and at the Horn of Africa Community Centre, in Melbourne's west. She says she would dearly love to bring her family to Melbourne but their applications have been rejected three times.

Hamdi almost didn't make it to Australia. As an 11-year-old living as a refugee in Egypt she had an inkling that she had family still in Somalia and when her 'aunt' received a visa to come to Australia with her family, Hamdi refused.

'The Australian embassy interviewed me and asked why I didn't want to go,' Hamdi said. 'My aunt had told them I had a boyfriend and that was why I didn't want to go. She thought the embassy might reject her if they found out I wasn't her daughter. So, she told me that I had to tell them I had a boyfriend and that was the reason I didn't want to go. She told me she would do something bad to me unless I told them that. I told the embassy people what she wanted because I was very scared of her. Sometimes I regret that because if I had told the truth, I might have my own family here with me now. But in Egypt I was only 11 and I had no one to help me. And if I had stayed there myself I would not have survived. I had no money and no family. I told the embassy I broke up with my boyfriend, I got a visa and I came to Australia.'

After spending time in women's refuges and in emergency housing, Hamdi was finally able to get on her feet and find work.

'I thank God that in Australia there are good people and a government that helps people. This is the reason I am here today,' she said.

CHAPTER 5
BOMBS, THREATS, EXECUTIONS
– LIFE UNDER ISIS

A Melbourne refugee family recently resettled here from Syria have told of the horror, barbarism and fear that became everyday life in an area controlled by ISIS extremists.

Syrian refugee Bassam said witnessing first-hand the brutality of ISIS death squads immediately sowed doubt in his mind about the long-term future for his family in their homeland. But a personal run-in with ISIS thugs in his hometown and the destruction of his house in a bombing — in the strife-torn and ISIS-controlled city of Raqqa — convinced him he must leave forever and get his family to safety.

Bassam witnessed the horror of the Syrian conflict up close when ISIS established a 'checkpoint' only a few hundred metres from his home. Syrian soldiers and anyone who spoke against ISIS would be held there and often executed. He told of one incident when, hearing something from his apartment one night, he went out onto the balcony to investigate.

'I was hiding as I looked and saw a ute bringing people to this checkpoint,' Bassam said. 'I realised they had two young soldiers, probably only about 18 years old, and they looked terrified.'

Bassam said a 'sheikh' was then called to come and decide what to do with the men. 'The sheikh simply ordered that the group cut the soldiers' throats.'

Bassam, who bought and sold cars in Raqqa, said his community lived in constant fear as ISIS had zero tolerance for anyone who spoke out against them. A tall fence around a nearby roundabout, once a busy intersection with cafes and restaurants, was displaying the heads of dead soldiers, he said. 'These people are brainwashed. They are just kids when they get involved in these groups,' Bassam said. 'They target the young, the poor and the uneducated.'

Bassam had his own run-in with the group when someone saw him smoking on the street one day. 'They grabbed me and locked me up for five hours because they said smoking is "against God". They said if they saw me smoking again, they would cut off my fingers.'

Apart from the threat of ISIS, Bassam and his family faced other dangers. As civilians living in a war zone, they almost became 'collateral damage'. He considers himself and his family lucky to be alive after their house was blown up.

'The bomb threw me across the room,' Bassam said. 'My wife was in the kitchen, she was pregnant at the time.'

Bassam's father returned home soon after to find the house completely destroyed. Together they eventually found all the family members alive under the rubble. That night, Bassam took his family to Turkey. The trip was a tense three-hour journey, with his wife heavily pregnant at the time.

'We drove as far as we could and then we had to walk a few kilometres to get across the border and we could hear guns being fired nearby,' Bassam said. 'At one point the Turkish troops were firing at us. I'm not sure how we survived but we made it to a safe place.'

The family was eventually resettled in Australia in early 2016.

Now Bassam, his wife and three children, all under five years of age, along with Bassam's parents are living in the Melbourne's north-west and have started new lives. However, the unimaginable things Bassam's family have witnessed have left indelible marks on them. His four-year-old son is traumatised and his mother blind in one eye.

'My son was so scared, he just stopped speaking after the house explosion. He has been seeing a psychologist since we came to Australia,' Bassam said. 'But he is improving and his English is good. He is making friends at kindergarten.'

Bassam said the explosion in the house left his mother blind in one eye, amongst other health conditions that she continues to face in Australia.

Bassam used to study law in Raqqa and hopes to continue his studies one day. But for now, he is focused on improving his English and his family's health.

'All Syrians wish the same thing, for Syria to go back to normal,' Bassam said. 'Syria used to be a safe country, a beautiful country. Like New York, it was the place that never sleeps.'

CHAPTER 6
RISING ABOVE TRAGEDY TO BECOME THE HEART AND SOUL OF A REFUGEE COMMUNITY

Karen Burmese refugee Evelyn Kunoo tells a heartbreaking story about her family that is emblematic of refugees across the world. Her sister's husband was killed fighting the Burmese Government leaving a widow and an infant son. A year later Evelyn's sister developed terminal leukaemia and asked her to look after the boy and, when he was old enough to understand, pass on to him his father's military uniform. Soon after, relatives from his father's family snatched the boy away. It was 20 years before Evelyn was able to find him — by then a grown man with his own family — and give him his father's uniform. As he unwrapped the package containing the clothing, out slid a letter written two decades earlier by his dying mother.

Her story is typical of the heartbreak and destruction that conflict and persecution inflicts on millions of refugee families across the globe. It represents a single teardrop in an ocean of sadness.

But Evelyn has risen above the tragedy of her people and the conflict that has caused their diaspora. She has become a leader and an example to her own community; a mother hen who has gathered her people around her and restored meaning to their lives.

Evelyn is the heart and soul of an extraordinary community garden project at Werribee Park, in Melbourne's west, that has seen the regeneration of an historic garden and — in a remarkable example of cultural cross-pollination — the blossoming of local refugee communities. What started as a call for volunteers to help rebuild the gardens turned into a therapy session for dislocated and isolated refugee families.

Werribee Park Area Chief Ranger James Brincat says Evelyn has played a central role in the success of the project titled 'Working Beyond the Boundaries', a collaboration between Parks Victoria and settlement agency AMES Australia. James says Evelyn has been responsible for bringing people from the local refugee communities into the garden and inspiring them to contribute.

'Evelyn is a leader in her community and she has become the heart and soul of the garden,' he said. 'She has recruited and organised the community members to work in the gardens and is a driving force behind the whole thing. What started out as community project to rebuild the old kitchen garden here at Werribee Mansion has turned out to be an incredibly successful social experiment and a model for other community engagement projects. Everyone involved in this is blown away by what we've achieved and the inspirational outcomes that have come from putting some seeds in the ground and seeing what happens — both literally and figuratively,' James said.

Evelyn said she felt responsible for her community and wanted to do something when she started to see rising levels of isolation and depression. When the opportunity to volunteer in the gardens came up, she jumped at it.

'The Karen people have a background in gardening and many of them were sitting at home with nothing to do,' she said. So we started coming here. At first it was just three or four women but soon more and more came. The Karen come here and they feel very good, very relaxed. And we can see a sense of achievement in growing things. Before people were sitting at home drinking and playing cards. For me this is about helping the Karen people. I want them to progress and succeed. I want to see them get better and make good lives for themselves. This program in the garden encourages them to work and to get out and do things and keep healthy.'

According to Parks Victoria, more than 200 people a week are now involved in the program. 'This has provided significant extra resources to the park allowing additional work to be completed and has provided a space for local communities to connect with others... while undertaking activities that range from gardening and cooking to weaving and handcrafts,' a Parks Victoria analysis says.

The experience gained as volunteers in the garden — thanks largely to Evelyn's efforts to get them there — has seen many members of local refugee communities obtain work in the region's commercial market gardens. One has even gained an apprenticeship as a park ranger with Parks Victoria.

With her humble background, litany of tragic family travails and her enduring good humour in the face of it all, Evelyn's life story reads like a Dickensian novel. She was born and lived until she was 14 in a small village in the Karen state in Burma. Both her parents died before she was eight; her mother when she was four and her father four years later. She had three sisters — one was adopted out and Evelyn has never been able to find who adopted her or where she is. From the age of eight, she had to work for her food — either as a cleaner or housekeeper and cook. 'I had no chance to study when I was young — I had to work,' she said.

Evelyn says that growing up in her village in Burma every person kept with them a small basket containing food, a cooking pot, spare clothes and personal items. 'All the time we used to have to run when the Burmese army came,' she said.

The ethnic minority Karen had been fighting a decades-long guerrilla war against the central government which had embarked on a campaign of ethnic cleansing systematically destroying and burning Karen villages.

When she was 14, Evelyn moved into the Karen Liberation Army central camp. In the camp she was supported by the fledgling Karen state authorities and learned to read and write. In 1984 with the war escalating, she moved to Mae La refugee camp on the Thai Burma border where she continued to study and learned nursing and midwifery. In the camp she also met and married her husband, Kert.

'Life in the camp was very hard. We were safe and we had food but we had no money and we were not allowed outside the camp,' Evelyn said.

Evelyn spent 22 years in the camp working as a nurse and midwife. She helped deliver babies, worked on women's health education programs including on HIV, and even distributed condoms while explaining what they were for.

'It was good to feel useful in the camp and to have some work because some people there had nothing — they were not even registered as refugees,' Evelyn said. But I always wanted a better life. I wanted a life not so much for me but for my children. When we first went into the camp we thought we would only be there a year.'

It would be two decades before she would leave and in that time she had five children. 'I always felt my children would have no future in the camp. It was not good for them because I wanted them to have the opportunity to learn and to have good lives,' Evelyn said.

She said the family was overjoyed when they learned they would be coming to Australia to be resettled as refugees. 'I was so happy. I knew my children would have a chance for a good education.'

But the journey to Australia presented its own challenges. 'I was very scared on the plane. I had never flown before and I thought it would fall out of the sky,' she said.

She and her family arrived in Sydney initially and didn't realise they had to catch a connecting flight to Melbourne. 'We thought we were in Melbourne but there was no one to meet us. I was very confused and we couldn't speak any English,' Evelyn said. Eventually they were helped by an airport worker and put on a later plane to Melbourne. Evelyn and her family were met by members of the Karen community in Melbourne and taken to live with a cousin in Werribee, on the city's western outskirts.

'It was very different, living in Australia,' she said. 'I had never seen a microwave oven before. Everything was different. We had never slept on mattresses before and for the first week, we slept on the floor. We didn't understand how to use the appliances or even how to open the gate at the front of the house. But the children were happy because we had been very poor refugees and they felt like we now had all these things.'

Evelyn's children have all gone on to higher education; her eldest son is a mechanic running his own business.

When not volunteering at Werribee Park or looking after her grandchildren, Evelyn and Kert love to get out into the bush. In keeping with their Karen heritage, they love to be close to nature. 'I love to visit the bush and wild places. I love the forests — they remind me of home,' she said.

After a lifetime of personal struggle and selfless work helping others, Evelyn finds peace in occasional solitude. 'It's very good to find quiet places where there are no people,' she said.

CHAPTER 7
FORCED TO FLEE A LIFETIME OF WORK: THE STORY OF A WWII VETERAN TURNED REFUGEE

Danial Haron's calloused and gnarled fingers tell the story of a life of hard, unremitting work. The 93-year-old Syrian refugee has seen trouble and hardship in his long life; he fought with the British army in WWII and he carved a productive farm out of a barren piece of land. But he says he has experienced nothing that compares with the bloodiness of the current conflict in Syria, nor the barbarous brutality of Islamic State.

After decades of work, Danial had a beautiful home, an abundant garden and a fertile wheat and sheep farm in the Christian village of Telbaoua, in north eastern Syria — just outside the city of Hasakah and 10 hours' drive from Damascus. In May 2015 ISIS came and destroyed his village.

'At 4am they came and burned the church and the fighting started. Some of us fled but others stayed and were captured,' Danial said, speaking through an interpreter. 'ISIS took them away and we don't know what happened to them.'

Danial's village had been left alone by ISIS until then. 'We were living in peace and minding our own business but that all changed when ISIS came that night,' he said.

Danial and his son Beniamen, 54, fled their farm on their tractor with only the clothes they were wearing. 'We left everything behind; a nice house, a fertile and productive farm and a good life,' Danial said. 'We lost everything — the work of 80 years. We also lost some of our friends. Some we have never seen or heard from again. It was a very hard time.'

Danial fought with the British army in Libya, Iran, Iraq and Palestine during the six years of WWII, enlisting at age 20 and sometimes fighting alongside Australians. 'There were soldiers from many countries with us; Polish, African, Indian and Australians — but we all wore the same uniform,' Danial said.

He said the current conflict was much worse than the war. 'Even the Germans treated civilians with respect,' Danial said. 'ISIS is much worse — they have no respect for anyone — they are thieves and murderers. ISIS is not human.'

Danial and Beniamin fled to Lebanon where they rented a small flat. They lived in limbo there for 14 months, struggling financially and registering with the UNHCR as refugees. With family already in Australia, they were selected for resettlement here and arrived in Melbourne in July 2016.

'I want to thank Australia. God bless this country,' Danial said.

He said he was looking forward to a peaceful life in Australia close to his family. 'We feel very welcome here. Everyone has been friendly. Everything is well organised here. There is a good health system. Everything works. When things are supposed to happen they happen — people don't let you down, not like in my country.'

He and Beniamin said they could not envisage going back to Syria. The fighting left much of Hasakah City in ruins and many surrounding villages, including Danial's, were completely destroyed.

'Even if peace returns to my country, I have nothing to go back to. Everything I had and knew was destroyed,' Danial said. 'I could never trust that Syria will be peaceful again.'

Beniamin, who taught commerce in Syria, says he plans to care for his father and eventually open a small business. 'I want to build a future and work to help other people,' he said.

CHAPTER 8
ESCAPE FROM THE 'KILLING FIELDS'
– A REFUGEE JOURNEY

Sitting on his father's shoulders walking through rice paddies littered with bodies left behind by brutal Khmer Rouge death squads, Hap Dan made a fateful journey to freedom and safety. For six long years his family had lived in the shadow of death, fearful that at any moment they might be denounced and executed on the spot as traitors to Pol Pot's 'utopian' revolution in Cambodia. Forced to leave their idyllic, simple life in the Cambodian countryside, they became part of the tide of humanity fleeing the notorious 'killing fields' genocide — eventually finding sanctuary in Australia.

Between 1979 and 1980 the communist Khmer Rouge regime under Pol Pot is estimated to have murdered as many as 2.2 million people while its social engineering and collectivisation policies turned the once lush and fertile Cambodian countryside into a wasteland.

'I lived through five or six years of the Khmer Rouge and the Vietnam War,' Hap recalled.

Now a 45-year-old father of three, Hap says the war was the first experience of his life. 'That is almost my earliest memory. But it was obviously not an ideal environment to grow up in,' he says euphemistically. 'Life back then is still very vivid for me, even now. I grew up in the countryside and we had sugar cane and corn fields, mango and banana trees and my parents ran small businesses. We made up our own toys and our own games. Life was very simple but it was a good life. We were barefoot and our water came from a village well. The neighbours would come over and we would cook things together. It was a happy time. I think my parents were doing well before the conflict, they had access to markets in Cambodia and in Vietnam.'

But he said that when the war came things changed.

'I remember my brothers used to go down to the river to play but one day one of our friends was blown up by a land mine. After that we were told not to go there,' Hap said.

He has surreal and vivid memories from his childhood in Cambodia.

'The Americans were carpet bombing with B52s and we could hear that sometimes,' Hap said. 'Often during the revolution we could hear fire fights and when the Khmer Rouge took control, things only got worse.'

His parents were forced to work on collective farms as part of Pol Pot's program to return the country to 'year zero'.

'If you were an intellectual, a teacher or a land-owner, you could be killed instantly or sent to die slowly from starvation in a labour camp. We lost family and friends this way. Mum and Dad had friends who just disappeared one day. They were taken away to a camp and never seen nor heard from again.'

He tells the story of how his mother was recognised as a 'bourgeois land owner' by a party official who had once lived in their village. But because his mother had once provided the official's family with food and clothes when they were in need, she was spared.

As time went by his parents realised they had to get their children out of Cambodia to provide them with safety and a chance at a future.

'We had a lot of close calls. One time we had bullets go through the house… so Mum and Dad made the decision to go then and there,' he said.

His parents were aware of the murderous excesses of the Khmer Rouge but kept the worst of the grisly details from their children.

'But we were living in it, there was no way of hiding it from the kids. As a young child born during this war we didn't know any different, we thought death, machine-gun battles and bombing were just a normal part of everyday life. Being so young and not of school age I had no other experience of life to compare it to. For Mum and Dad, it was all about protecting us; giving us a future. So, they just left everything behind to get us out,' he said.

His family split up on the journey to safety with himself and two brothers travelling with his father and his mother and other siblings leaving separately.

'We travelled by road at night walking to the border of Thailand. We walked past rice paddies and sometimes through jungle. There were bodies everywhere,' Hap said. 'The Khmer Rouge or an army unit would just come through an area and leave the dead behind.'

His father and mother were reunited in Thailand and after six months in camps, they were processed for resettlement in a third country.

'We were given the option of going to the US or Canada but because dad had a cousin in Melbourne, he decided we would come to Australia,' he said.

That was in 1980 and even though he was only six, Hap remembers the sense of cultural dislocation.

'I remember on the plane we were served airline food in foil pouches. We didn't know what it was,' he said. 'Mum had bought some bananas to take on the trip to Australia but they wouldn't let her take them on the plane. She spoke no English and I think the immigration officials had trouble making her understand that there would be food and everything else she needed. But she was so used to fending for herself and her family that she wouldn't believe them.'

In Australia his father found work with his cousin at the Victoria Markets while his mother stayed home to look after Hap and his six siblings.

Hap says although no one knew much about post-traumatic stress disorder back then, his parents and their compatriots suffered from it. 'I remember once the Channel 7 chopper went overhead and my dad and his friends made us all run away... it was a number of years before my father became relaxed about helicopters,' he said.

Hap, who lives in Melbourne's east and works in employment services, says his parents believe their decision to leave Cambodia was the best they ever made.

'Coming to Australia was a trip into the unknown for my parents but if we had stayed who knows what would have happened?' he said. 'My parents were always motivated by their kids' welfare and future and doing what they did gave all of us a chance at having good lives. Now most of us have our own kids and there are even grandkids — all of these young lives are a vindication of what my parents did. My mum is still around and has managed to experience her first great grandchild. Unfortunately, my dad passed away recently before he got to meet his great grandson, following years of ill health contributed to by the hardship he experienced during the Khmer Rouge/Vietnam war.

'There were many nights since coming to Australia where I would hear my dad scream out and cry in pain during his sleep, as the ghosts and trauma of the war continued to haunt him. In the end he was at peace and passed away in the night after saying his good byes to us kids.

'To this day I consider both of my parents as my heroes for the sacrifice they made to get us to safety so we all could have a chance in life.

'In the end, for us, it was all about family.'

CHAPTER 9
CONFLICT, CANCER AND CRUELTY
– A REFUGEE FAMILY'S JOURNEY

Escaping a desperate gun battle, beating breast cancer in a war zone and living for months in a cramped single room in the middle of a foreign city are all parts of the amazing story of one refugee family who escaped one of the most brutal conflicts in modern history to find safety in Melbourne.

The Gharibeh family had decent lives in the Syrian capital of Damascus — running a business, attending school and entertaining friends — until war came.

When the shells started pounding the contested districts of their hometown, their lives — like the bricks and masonry of the city said to be the oldest in the world — started to disintegrate.

Antoun Gharibeh, his wife and three children saw everything they had worked towards shattered in just a few short months.

'It was about five years ago when the war started in Syria that we first began to feel fearful. The shelling started and there was fighting and we felt under threat,' Antoun said, speaking though his interpreter and Melbourne-based brother-in-law Ramez Aldaoud. 'The school my kids went to was bombed so we stopped sending them. Business became difficult so we started to lose our income and there was the physical threat as the fighting started to increase and spread.'

Antoun and his family lived in a largely Christian suburb of Damascus but his carpentry and joinery business was in another district where there was more intense fighting. As the war escalated it became more difficult to operate the business but Antoun would occasionally go to check on the premises. On one of these trips he was captured by an anti-government militia group.

'I was being held by these gunmen and I was very scared,' Antoun said.

But just as he began to fear the worst, a government patrol appeared and a fire fight broke out allowing Antoun to take cover in a ditch and slowly crawl away from the gun battle.

'I was terrified. It was chaos and I was trying to keep down to avoid being hit but also trying to crawl away,' Antoun said.

Antoun says he crawled six blocks to escape the battle and finally made his way to a government checkpoint from where he was able to get aboard an army convoy vehicle and make his way home.

'I approached the checkpoint with my hands raised saying "I am fleeing the militia". But I did not know at first whether they would believe me or how I would be treated. I told them my story and luckily they believed me,' he said.

Antoun's brother-in-law Ramez explained that people in the west are told that the government of Bashir al-Assad are the bad guys and the militias are fighting for freedom. 'But if you are a Christian in Syria, things are a lot more complicated than that,' Ramez said. 'Many of the Islamic groups are suspicious of Christians so it can be very dangerous.'

When Antoun arrived home the evening of his brush with militias, he told his wife, Amal, of his lucky escape and they decided together it was time to leave the country of their birth.

'We decided we must go "yesterday and before tomorrow",' Antoun said, using an old Syrian phrase to emphasise the family's desperation.

The family hired a taxi and headed for the Lebanese border with their hearts in their mouths.

'It was a risky trip but luckily there were no militia checkpoints on the route our driver took,' Antoun said.

Arriving in Beirut with little more than the clothes they wore and very little money, they stayed with Antoun's brother in a single room for two months until they were able to rent a small apartment outside Beirut. With little money and no assets, they were forced to appeal to family members in Australia for help.

'It was very hard for us and we received very little help from the UNHCR. Without the help from our family in Australia, I don't know what we would have done,' Antoun said.

The Gharibeh family's relatives in Australia had already applied to have them come here as refugees when Amal fell ill with breast cancer.

This put the whole process back 12 months because of the Australian Government's health requirements for refugees and migrants. And because of the cost of health care in Beirut, Noor was forced to travel back to Syria for treatment.

'It was very stressful,' Amal's sister and Ramez' wife Noor Haddad said. 'They could not afford for Amal to have treatment in Lebanon because it would have cost $US100,000 — so she had to go back to Damascus for an operation and for chemotherapy,' Noor said. 'It was very dangerous and it meant that it took much longer to get them to Australia.'

Antoun, Amal and their children, George, 11, Jolyana, 10, and Jouly, 3, arrived in Melbourne in June 2016 after three years in limbo in Lebanon. Amal is fully recovered from her cancer and the family is now living with Ramez and Noor at their home in Melbourne's northern suburbs.

Antoun and Amal are relieved to be safe after their five-year ordeal and are optimistic about the future for themselves and their children who started school in the local area this week.

'In Damascus the children were very scared and could not sleep. They could not go to school because of the shelling,' Antoun said. 'Also we were scared for them all of the time. Until now they have not been to school for four years. I feel safe here and I'm very thankful to Australia to be here and for the assistance my family has received. Just seeing the happiness on my children's faces tells me they now have a chance at a brilliant future — something they would not have had if we had stayed in the Middle East.'

CHAPTER 10
THE BUSINESS OF SETTLING IN TO A NEW COMMUNITY

For Eritrean refugee Nadia Hassan, Australia has truly proved to be the land of opportunity. The mother of three has built a thriving import and retail business in the heart of multicultural Footscray, in Melbourne's west. She says that hard work, persistence and an eye for market gaps have been the secrets to her success.

'I came to Australia from Eritrea as a refugee in 1988. I came because there was a war there. It was a very bad situation and I could not stay in my country,' Nadia said.

She says she and her family, and thousands of others, were forced to leave behind their homes and their way of life.

Eritrea has been wracked by a succession of civil wars since the 1960s as it first sought independence from Ethiopia and then as conflicts arose between rival independence groups within Eritrea.

Yet another war beset the region in May 1998 and June 2000 as Eritrea and Ethiopia clashed over a territory dispute. A final peace accord was only agreed to in 2018, twenty years after the initial confrontation.

All of these conflicts are estimated to have left hundreds of thousands dead and cost half a billion dollars in one of the world's poorest regions.

'I spent some time in a refugee camp and when I came to Australia there was a language barrier for me. So, I decided I needed to learn English and I did some courses,' Nadia said. 'After a few months I started work. I worked in factories and hotels and I always wanted to save money to start my own business. At the beginning I started importing some lines of foods that I knew I could sell in my community here. We started small at first and built the business up slowly. It took a long time before we became truly successful but we never gave up.'

Nadia started importing food lines from Africa and the Middle East for her community. Her business has grown and now she imports food products from across the globe as well as health and beauty lines. Her Paisley street shop stocks special flours and dried fruits and spices.

'Because we built the business slowly we gained a lot of knowledge over 20 years,' she said.

Now she runs a shop and import business in Paisley Street in the centre of Footscray. She has three children — two at university and one completing high school.

'I came as a refugee and initially life was very hard but I always knew what I wanted to do,' Nadia said. 'I always had the thought of having my own business and so I saved up and first I opened a milk bar. Then I worked hard and built up the business and now I am financially secure and I have brought up my children and I feel good about what I have achieved. Running the business has made me feel part of the community. I feel very settled here now — this is my home. Now I feel very about good about what I have done in my life. I feel lucky to be here in Australia and to have the opportunity to do something that I wanted to do. I wish the best of luck to everyone who comes to this country. Australia has opportunities for anyone if you are prepared to work hard and if you have an idea. Whatever I have done, it is possible for anyone to do; you just need a bit of commitment and hard work — that's all.'

CHAPTER II
NEW SCHOOL ENGLISH PROGRAM REACHES OUT TO PARENTS

A group of Karen refugee parents are receiving English lessons at the school their children attend in an innovative new scheme to improve outcomes for both them and their children. The pilot project is being supported by settlement agency AMES Australia at Laverton College P-12 in Melbourne's west. The College's principal Richard Jones launched the initiative after seeing a need to improve communication between parents and the school and also an opportunity to improve educational and employment outcomes for both his students and their parents. The program has started with a group of Karen refugee parents at Laverton but if its early promise is any guide, it might be rolled out more broadly.

Mr Jones said face to face conversation was a key component of learning.

'One of the expectations that we have is that kids are able to go home and read to their parents pretty much every night. Now our Karen kids will be able to do that and their parents will be able to understand what they're reading and to be able to connect to maybe the story or the information,' he said. 'If it's a text from some science work or enquiry work, and then the kids will be able to explain to their parents a little more about it; there will some conversation around it and it's building that habit with our kids. Being a prep to year twelve school we've got the opportunity for kids to be here for twelve years and some families are here for all of that time so we want to build the skills of our children as well as their families and the parents.'

The program grew out of Mr Jones seeing a group of parents who were dependent on translators when he first came to the school.

'There was a whole group of those parents including the Karen who were not connecting with school in an authentic sort of way,' he said. 'So I wanted to make that connection more genuine and language is the key to interaction. We can have translators and we can translate as much information as we want — and we do —'our newsletters and other documents are translated into Karen. But to build the capacity of those parents and then build the capacity of those parents to get better jobs and then provide better outcomes for their children required some work around English language. So this course particularly focuses on interview skills, application, the writing, and then the practicing of those to enable the parents to achieve better employment outcomes which will then benefit the children.'

He said there had been a positive response among the parents:

'We started in term three last year and had a regular group of parents attend all term. That's two days a week, two hours for each session, so four hours in total. They continued all of term three so we continued into term four and now we are continuing into this year,' Mr Jones said. 'Language acquisition is slow but we know we are making some progress. It's about building trust with the parents and to enable that trust to continue in an authentic way — and often that's around parents expressing some concerns that they may have in their own language and having those listened to by the parents' teacher,' he said.

Mr Jones said its rich cultural diversity was both an asset and a challenge for his school and that the parents' English program was a way of building connections between ethnic groups.

'We do have a large number of Karen families and then we have a large number of Arabic families as well as some Islander families from Samoa, and some North African families,' he said. 'These groups work well together in the school and language is a barrier so we are looking at maybe expanding this model to include some other groups that could work with AMES to improve outcomes for those families as well.'

Mr Jones said part of the rationale for introducing the program was a belief that teaching English to the parents of students ultimately benefits the students as well.

'We firmly believe this is the case. We see that the Karen parents are well connected with the school and their own community but we'd like them to be connected to the broader school community as well,' he said. 'So that would mean some other groups within the school. Their children are very respectful. If you walk around the school now you'll see the whole school, all of those groups of people working well together. It's calm, it's orderly, and they're on task. We just need the language skill to improve so that the outcomes for our children and their children are greater.

'Many of the students that come to us might come in year five or ten, with very low language skills. In the end that means they are not going to be able to achieve the same outcomes unless we improve their language skills very quickly. So we've worked on a model with an EAL consultant that we brought in last year, that is intervention within the class, and it's targeted work around oral literacy; it's also combining with some work from some other expert partners that we've done and that's very explicit around students understanding the meaning of one sentence and then taking that meaning and seeing what the second sentence adds to that meaning and then the paragraph and then what does the second paragraphs add to my understanding of the first paragraph.

'It's about vocab equalling knowledge and kids working through that. Our teachers have grasped on to this pretty quickly because it's a very effective way of pacing a lesson and to gauge students understanding within the class. So, every hour students are expected to be able to say "I now know" what they didn't know an hour ago. I think the kids like that because they're seeing that there is progress being made very quickly. Where language skill is still weakest, maybe in writing maybe sometimes in reading comprehension, there will be students that are withdrawn from class. There are additional classes before school and we are looking at whether we need to progress towards a Saturday school for some students.'

Mr Jones said that ultimately the program was aimed at improving educational and employment opportunities for the whole school community.

'If we are talking about the state average being at one point and our school being somewhere below that we need to be closer to that state average very quickly to enable our students to have better outcomes and be able to get the sort of jobs that other kids are getting, study courses that other kids are able to and have experiences that others have,' he said.

CHAPTER 12
SAVING A CULTURE FROM EXTINCTION

Yuhana Nashmi recently spent three months journeying around Iran, Iraq and Turkey recording the few remaining speakers of an ancient language, photographing crumbling manuscripts and documenting artefacts and sacred objects under threat of destruction. Yuhana's work is part of a unique and far-sighted program to preserve and document the fast disappearing ancient culture and traditions of the Mandaean people. In the years since Iraq's descent into sectarian chaos the Mandaeans have become targets for both ISIS — as 'infidel non-believers' — and also the Shia militias because of their pacifist beliefs and reluctance to take up arms against ISIS.

Caught in the middle of this bitter and interminable conflict many Mandaeans have perished; thousands more have fled their ancient homelands as refugees. This diaspora has put at risk the very social and cultural fabric of this pre-Christian ethno-religious group whose rich language and traditions predate the Bible.

Yuhana, a Mandaean himself, says about 85 per cent of his people have now left Iraq and Iran. There are just 10 families in Melbourne but a thriving community of about 10,000 in Sydney. There are larger communities of exiles in the US, UK, Sweden and Canada although the global population numbers just 40-50,000.

The Mandaeans are an ethno-religious community indigenous of southern Mesopotamia, often described by scholars as 'the last Gnostics from the ancient antiquity'. They are among the world's oldest, smallest and least known religious communities. They have become the unintended victims of the American invasion of Iraq and the civil war that followed in its aftermath. As Gnostics, they have a dualistic view of life, which encompasses both good and evil and faith which is based on personal experience and pacifism. This pacifist outlook has made them targets for other groups.

Before the 2003 US invasion, more than 50,000 Mandaeans lived in Iraq; by 2011, the population had dropped to around 3,500, according to Human Rights Watch. They are now considered one of the world's most vulnerable peoples.

Mandaeans in Iraq have been killed, kidnapped or forced to convert to Islam, says Yuhana, who now lives in Sydney.

'Mandaeans traditionally are very peaceful people, very learned; they traditionally work as doctors, engineers, teachers and silver and goldsmiths. In fact, the word 'manda' in Aramaic means knowledge,' he said. 'But the Mandaeans are heading for extinction in their traditional homelands. Simply, a Mandaean lives in fear nowadays in Iraq.'

Threatened by the militants of the Islamic State as well as by Shia paramilitary groups and local authorities, the Mandaeans, who are religiously prohibited from taking up arms to defend themselves, often felt they had nowhere to turn. Some have received messages in the form of a single bullet in an envelope and given 24 hours to leave the country. Thousands are languishing in refugee camps in the countries surrounding Iraq and Syria, where they live in difficult conditions.

It was these circumstances that prompted Yuhana to join a project run out of Exeter University in the UK, which seeks to preserve and document endangered cultures.

'This is a three-year project and we are collecting the recordings of the Mandaean language — a form of Aramaic — books, documents and artefacts to try to preserve Manadean culture and traditions,' he said.

Yuhana, who is trained in Mandaean religion and language, went to Iraq and Iran recently and visited towns and villages where Mandaeans live as a field researcher although on a tourist visa.

'Mandaean culture and language is effectively banned in Iran — you are not allowed to name your children with Mandaean names — and few people there still speak the language; so that was why I went there to record them,' he said. 'I interviewed people and priests. We recorded the details of sacred objects and photographed manuscripts and talked to people about the issues they face. The biggest concern is that the Mandaeans are not acknowledged in the Iranian constitution as 'Ahl Al

Kitab' or 'People of the Book', which has serious consequences for them.'

The aim of the project is to create an online archive that will preserve the heritage and culture of the Mandaeans. The archive, which will be publicly accessible, will store recordings, manuscripts, transcripts of interviews and photographs.

'The aim of the project is to preserve the culture, mythology and folklore of the Mandaeans,' Yuhana said. The purpose is, most importantly, to prevent this endangered heritage being lost, but we also hope the public will be better informed about the Mandaeans.'

He said that Mandaean communities here in Australia and around the world are also grappling with the problem of preserving their own unique culture.

'Mandaeans traditionally have been insular — even though you would once have found them in many towns and villages in Iraq. Many of the traditions are a little at odds with a western lifestyle and people usually didn't marry outside the community. So, discussions have begun in the community about how some of these things might change. The community is having a debate socially, religiously, culturally on how to redefine things. The priests are trying, and the educated people are trying, to revisit the texts and interpret things differently,' Yuhana said.

In his travels Yuhana came across what he believes is the last working Mandaean boat-builder on the Tigris River at Amarah, in southern Iraq.

'Once there were hundreds of Mandaeans building boats. It is sad they have almost all gone. But if we are going to preserve our culture and history we need to find new ways; we need to reinterpret who we are and apply our belief systems to the societies in which we now find ourselves,' he said. 'We as a people have been collectively traumatised by this chaos that has been led by some powerful people in the world! We feel like we were caught in the middle of this for no reason other than destroying everything beautiful in Iraq!'

CHAPTER 13
FEEDING A PASSION FOR SELF-RELIANCE

It's the lunch time rush in an eatery at Campbellfield in Melbourne's north and an Australian couple sits in the window seat sharing a plate of kebabs; a Chinese family is sitting in a back corner eating pulao rice and two Turkish men in fluoro jackets are drinking lassis. Welcome to the Afghan Kebab Restaurant, an establishment opened recently by three asylum seekers serving traditional central Asian cuisine. The trio pooled their money and borrowed more from friends to lease and fit out the premises, which sits presciently across the road from the former Ford factory.

The partnership is just one example of how dozens of asylum seekers across Australia are opening businesses and employing others once they are granted work rights.

Restaurant partner and front of house manager Esmatullah Hakimi says he was prompted to open the business after knee injuries left him unable to do labouring work. And after two months the restaurant is full each day for lunch and dinner and there are plans for a second business.

'I am so happy. We are more successful than I had hoped for. We ran out of supplies in the first week and had to order more,' Mr Hakimi says.

The business now employs another 12 people, including Afghans, Arabs, Iranians, and Indians. Mr Hakimi, 32, says his customers include a wide spread of ethnicities who call the local area home.

'We have everyone come here... Europeans, Asians, Chinese, Arabs, Turks...' he said. 'Most people come to try the food for the first time and become loyal customers.'

Mr Hakimi said that when his injuries precluded him from labouring work, he looked for another way to earn a living. 'I didn't want to sit around doing nothing and getting handouts from Centrelink. I wanted to support myself and my family,' he said.

In Afghan culture there is a code of honour — 'we don't like freeloaders'.

Mr Hakimi works from 9am until 11pm, sometimes seven days a week. He says he is driven to provide for his wife and two children and also to provide work for people in similar circumstances to his own.

'I would love to open more restaurants so I can hire more people even if there might be less profit,' he said.

Mr Hakimi's circumstances are not dissimilar to the 30,000 or so asylum seekers who have come to Australia fleeing persecution, conflict, torture or worse.

The ethnic Hazara was a science teacher in Afghanistan but because his school was supported by a Christian charity, he was branded a heretic by the Taliban and was forced to flee to Iran.

'The Taliban said we could not teach science but only preach Islam. And because we were supported by a Christian group, we were accused of preaching Christianity,' Mr Hakimi said. 'I was ambushed by the Taliban twice but managed to escape. I was told the Taliban was after me and that I should leave. I went to Iran but I was there illegally and there were problems with the Iranian police so I went back to Afghanistan.'

With his life still under threat in his homeland, in 2010 Mr Hakimi travelled to Malaysia, Indonesia and then by boat to Christmas Island. He spent 20 months in immigration detention before he was released and his family joined him in 2013. He now has refugee status in Australia but his partners are asylum seekers on bridging visas. Mr Hakimi says the business was four years in the making.

'It took me four years to understand how to run a food business in Australia. In Afghanistan I would know the city and market and it is much easier to open a shop,' he said. 'Here it is very different setting up a business. There is registration, hygiene standards... you need an ABN number.'

Mr Hakimi says that despite the long hours, the worry and the debt, his gamble on a business is worth it.

'I want to make a success of this business for myself and my family but also so I can employ people from the same background as me. They also need the chance to be independent and to make good lives for themselves.'

CHAPTER 14
REFUGEE DOCTOR'S STORY OF COURAGE AND PERSISTENCE

Associate Professor Munjed Al Muderis' life changed the day he was ordered by soldiers to surgically remove the ears of Iraqi defectors in Baghdad after his chief surgeon was shot for refusing.

Fleeing to Australia as a refugee, Munjed spent months at Curtin Detention Centre in Western Australia waiting to be processed; a time he says was one of the lowest points in what he calls the wheel of life. Munjed recounts his journey from asylum seeker to world-leading osseointegration expert in his heartbreaking and inspiring memoir, *Walking Free*.

From his time as a boy in Iraq, to professional strides in Australia, Munjed's life has been one of hardship, courage and strength.

Munjed was born in 1972 to an agnostic aristocratic family in Baghdad, but experienced the turmoil of his country from a young age when the war with Iran broke out in 1980. As an 8-year-old in 1981 he was nearly killed by machine gun fire from an Iranian fighter plane in Baghdad.

Though the war changed the very way of life in Baghdad, Munjed refused to give up on his dream of becoming a surgeon. During his studies at medical school, he met his first wife and was married by the time he was 23. However, after irreconcilable differences in religious beliefs and values, the couple were divorced within a year.

Conflict surrounded Munjed's life as the dictatorship of Saddam Hussein tore Iraq apart.

'Unless you've lived under a brutal dictatorship in a country whose economy has virtually collapsed, it would be hard to imagine what life was like in Iraq in the late 1990s. Without question, it was a terrible place to live in those years,' Munjed wrote in his memoir. '... every Iraqi knew that you didn't challenge the regime — or even encourage the impression that you might question it. Blind obedience was required and the consequences of not following the Saddam line were awful.'

After studying medicine at Baghdad University, Munjed began his first-year residency in 1999 and encountered those consequences first hand.

In Iraq military service was compulsory, and Saddam issued an order that all deserters would be punished with disfigurement.

One morning, Saddam's henchmen rounded up army deserters and brought them to the hospital where Munjed worked, in order to get the doctors to disfigure the deserters by surgically removing the tops of their ears. The most senior doctor refused as he had sworn an oath to do no intentional harm to his patients. As a result, he was promptly marched to the carpark, briefly interrogated and shot in front of medical staff, including Munjed.

Munjed, forced with no other options besides death or compliance, hid in the women's toilet cubicle for hours and planned his escape from Iraq.

'I didn't know how I could keep one step ahead of the Iraqi authorities, but I did know that if they caught me, I would face intense — and potentially brutal — interrogation before the ultimate sanction of death,' Munjed wrote.

With the help of friends, Munjed managed to flee to Jordan before making his way to Indonesia via Abu Dhabi and Malaysia. From Java he crammed onto a boat with 150 other asylum seekers bound for Christmas Island, all with hopes of starting new lives for themselves. During the difficult and dangerous journey Munjed used his medical skills to treat fellow passengers, including several pregnant women who were suffering from severe sea sickness.

After his long journey to escape persecution, he found himself in immigration in detention, locked up, in solitary confinement and was known only by a number.

Finally, after 10 months, Munjed was freed after being recognised as a refugee, and began another long journey to obtain his Australian medical qualifications.

Now, after working from Canberra to Mildura and studying extensively, Munjed is an orthopaedic robotic limb surgeon and a clinical lecturer at Macquarie University and The Australian School of Advanced Medicine. He is one of the world's leading osseointegration surgeons, fulfilling his dream of transforming the lives of amputees through world-leading technology that allows them to walk again.

In 2014 Munjed watched one of his patients, 24-year-old British soldier Rifleman Michael Swain, walk towards Queen Elizabeth II to receive his MBE using perfectly functioning artificial robotic legs.

'It was a particularly poignant moment for me, because I knew the heartbreak and courage that had brought him to this ceremony,' Munjed said.

After having his legs blown off by a makeshift bomb while serving in Afghanistan, Michael was fitted with traditional socket prostheses that caused so many difficulties that he became mostly restricted to a wheelchair. It wasn't until after extensive research on the internet that Michael found Munjed and begun his journey to walking like he once had.

'I like what I do because it's changing people's lives. It integrates them back into society by bringing amputees as close as possible back to normality,' Munjed said.

Without Munjed's persistence and courage he may have never made it to Australia and been given the opportunity to provide his patients with a new lease on life.

Munjed, who now lives in Sydney with his wife Irina and their daughter Sophia, said he decided to write his memoir because it's a story that's worth telling. 'I made it through my experiences because I have a very strong will and am a positive person. Many people can't make it through because they don't have the education and positivity that I have,' he said.

Munjed believes the refugee story is one often told for refugees, rather than by them.

'The media in Australia isn't the most fair as it involves a lot of misinformation and bias. *Walking Free* was created in order to tell the story from the perspective of someone who has actually been through it,' he said. 'Atrocities have been and are still committed in the Middle East due to lack of education, fanaticism, religion and power-hungry people. It's a very complex situation. The more we educate people about what's going on, then change will happen from the grassroots.'

Walking Free is a part of that education as it provides a small, accessible window to the public about the past, present and possible future of the Middle East and the treatment of refugees in Australia.

'Australians need to know about the struggles that people face in the Middle East, as well as what happens once they come here. I think the tide of the opinion of the Australian public is changing. They are realising that refugees are humans and that they are suffering,' Munjed said. 'Australians are good people by nature and by understanding what has happened in the past we can fix what's happening in the Middle East.'

CHAPTER 15
SYRIAN REFUGEES BETWEEN A ROCK AND A HARD PLACE

As civil war engulfed his homeland in 2012 Syrian refugee Kifarkis Nissan's call up for army service left him with an appalling choice; join the military and risk his family being killed by rebel militias — or refuse to serve and be jailed.

Instead, Kifarkis took a third option — he fled his homeland and found relative safety in a refugee camp in Lebanon.

Now settled in Melbourne Kifarkis says he is one of the lucky ones to have found a safe place to rebuild his life.

'There are still four million people displaced from Syria. My family and I are very lucky to be here in Australia,' he said.

As Christians, Kifarkis and his family were in grave danger as Islamic State (ISIS) took control of vast swathes of the Syrian countryside.

They were part of an Assyrian Christian community living in more than 30 villages strung out along the Khabur River in northern Syria close to the border with Turkey.

The Khabur River is a tributary of the Euphrates one of the major sources of water in a region which once was home to one of the oldest civilisations on Earth. It is part of fertile plain that is irrigated by a series of dams and canals.

It is also an area that was once controlled by ISIS. The villages are now empty and their 30,000-or-so inhabitants have either fled or been killed.

'They burned down all our churches, they kidnapped people. It was a terrible time for us,' Kifarkis said.

In February 2015 ISIS again attacked the Assyrian villages killing many and kidnapping hundreds more.

'They were asking ransom of $US10,000 per person when an average salary is about $US100 a month. So it was impossible for people to pay,' he said.

The former agricultural engineer says Christians and other minority groups were caught in the middle when fighting erupted between government forces, ISIS and other rebel militias.

'Christians were out on a limb. We were not with the government; we were not with the rebels and everyone discriminated against us. Often we didn't know which group the people threatening us were from,' he said. 'I did not want to take sides; I did not want to take up weapons so when I got the letter from the army saying I must join them it put me in a very bad position. Where we live there are rebel groups who oppose the army, so if I joined the army I would have been leaving my family in danger. If I didn't join, the army would come for me.'

The day he received the letter and realising the invidious position he was in, he took his family across the border into Lebanon. But Kifarkis still has family members in refugee camps in Lebanon and others struggling to survive in neighbouring countries.

He says he is very grateful to the Australian Government for taking an extra 12,000 refugees from the Syrian conflict.

'The Australian Government is protecting refugees and that is good. We have the chance to build a new life and our children will be safe and they can get an education. We are very grateful for these things,' Kifarkis said.

After studying English for a year, Kifarkis now works as a Community Liason Officer with torture and trauma counselling organisation Foundation House.

'We want to work and serve this country because this country is protecting us,' he said. 'We feel welcome here. People respect out religion and culture. We feel equal and that gives me encouragement.'

CHAPTER 16
REFUGEE'S ORDEAL SPARKS A PASSION FOR JUSTICE AND FAIRNESS

The last time refugee Mehdi Hassani saw his brother alive he was running for his life through unfamiliar streets on the outskirts of the Afghan town of Shindand with armed kidnappers in pursuit. The pair had been bundled into a car with bags placed over their heads as they walked out of the airport terminal after a short holiday.

'I had been on a holiday with my brother and as we walked out of the airport a car came up and offered us a lift. But before we could react we were put into the car and blindfolded at gunpoint,' Mehdi said. 'The car drove for about an hour and then it stopped. They — I think they may have been Taliban or criminals — made us get out of the car and push. I was talking to my brother saying that if we did not get away we would probably end up dead. So, we both ran away pulling the bags off out heads as we ran. They fired at us as we ran. I didn't know where I was and I lost sight of my brother.'

He finally made it to safety but Mehdi says he never saw his brother again.

'We don't know what happened to him and my family still doesn't know,' he said.

Mehdi said that in the weeks that followed his parents received threatening phone calls.

'The calls were from people saying "we have you son — bring us the other one or we will kill him". My parents told me that I should leave the country — they said they had lost one son and didn't want to lose another.'

Mehdi said his family were still receiving the calls months after the incident.

'They have to keep moving houses to stay safe,' he said.

He said he was targeted because he had an IT job with a foreign-owned construction company.

Mehdi paid a people smuggler $US12,000 to get him to Indonesia. There he applied for and was granted a humanitarian refugee visa through the United Nations and arrived in Australia in November 2014.

His experience of corruption and lawlessness in his home country has instilled in him a passion to become a police officer.

'I see what happens in my country and it makes me angry and sad. In Afghanistan there is no law and no justice. If you are strong you can do what you want and if you are poor you can do nothing,' he said. 'I want to become a police officer in Australia. I want to uphold the law. This is a good country where things are fair and everyone is equal in the law. Coming to Australia has saved my life and I am grateful for that. I would like to do something to give back and to make a contribution to the country.'

He has improved his English with lessons at migrant refugee settlement agency AMES and completed a first aid course. He is about to start a lifesaving course and plans to study for a Certificate IV in Justice at TAFE before applying to join the Victoria Police. He has been helped by his AMES teachers and counsellor to identify a pathway to help him achieve his goals.

'I know what I need to do to achieve my dream of becoming a police officer and I am on that pathway and I am determined to get there,' Mehdi said.

CHAPTER 17
REFUGEE'S SMILE HIDES LONG AND TORTUOUS JOURNEY TO SAFETY

Blinded by a land mine explosion, exiled from his boyhood village by a brutal military regime and after more than 20 years stuck in a camp for the displaced, Karen-Burmese refugee Ngo Way still finds reasons to smile.

He has found refuge in Australia and is learning English with the help of a volunteer tutor though settlement agency AMES — while witnessing his five young children grow up. He arrived after spending more than 20 years behind razor wire in cramped and sodden conditions in a refugee camp on the Thai-Burma border and he and his wife Hla Win are slowly rebuilding their lives.

Ngo and thousands of others like him are refugees from the conflict in Burma which has seen the Burmese government and military persecute minority ethnic groups, attacking and burning their villages. There are an estimated 150,000 Karen living in camps along the Thai-Burma border.

As a young teenager Ngo was abducted by the military, marched away and forced to work as a porter.

'In the village I studied Karen but in Burma you are not allowed to study Karen so the soldiers would come along and take people away,' he said.

He finally left his village in 1984 when he and his family were forced to flee as the Burmese army approached.

'The soldiers came to the village and we ran away. We slept in the jungle and we walked for two weeks to get to the border,' Ngo said.

Living in the camp with food scarce, Ngo and his friends would often scavenge for vegetables in nearby forests. He was on such a search when he was blinded by a land mine.

'One day in 1996 we snuck outside the camp to look for vegetables. I stepped on a stick and it accidentally triggered a mine nearby. I was with three friends but I was the only one hurt. I was blinded and lost hearing on my left side,' he said.

Ngo spent a month in hospital before being sent back to the refugee camp unable to see anything. He says life in the camp was difficult without sight and he was forced to stay at home while his wife Hla Win tried to earn extra money for the family.

'In the camp there were a lot of people but I could not go far. I just stayed at home to look after the children. I had no job and no opportunity to do anything or to study,' he said.

But he said coming to Australia has given him and his family a new lease of life.

'Now my children can get a better education and have more opportunities,' Ngo said. 'It is easier to move around here and there are places I can go — not like the camp. And I feel safe for myself and my family. It is good to be here. I am happy.'

One of the key factors in his optimism is the support he has been given by volunteers and community organisations.

He and his wife have been helped by AMES Australia community guide Say Gay, a former Karen refugee herself. Gay has helped the family with things like doctors' appointments, shopping and schooling; seemingly everyday tasks but daunting ones if you don't speak the local language and are not familiar with its customs.

The family also has an AMES volunteer English tutor in Michele O'Connell, who is helping Ngo and Hla learn English. Michele says volunteering is 'chicken soup for my soul'.

'I always make sure I have enough time for my refugees. And I am still in touch with most of my previous students,' said Michele, who has been volunteering for ten years. 'One couple I tutored have just bought their own home — they're doing really well and it's great to see. It's rewarding to see people flourish and get on with their lives. I started volunteering when my own kids were babies. It was tricky but it was something I wanted to do so we juggled things. One of my first students was terrified to go out in public alone because she was afraid she couldn't speak English. Now she's working in a bakery and she's driving — taking her kids to school. I love seeing the difference you can make in people's lives. It's fantastic,' she said.

She says all of her students have visited her home.

'We've had things like Australia Day celebrations with lamb chops on the barbecue,' she said. It's been wonderful to share those times with the students and it's important for my kids to realise how lucky they are.'

Because of his vision impairment, Michele faces extra challenges in helping Ngo learn English. But she uses some 'tricks of the trade' to help him along.

'It's really different and much more challenging than teaching a sighted person but it's not impossible,' Michele said. 'We use letters glued to a board and a set of loose letters. And an iPad is really handy for repeating the alphabet. But I feel I get more out of volunteering than I give. It's very, very rewarding.'

AMES Volunteer Coordinator Gitta Clayton says it is easy to underestimate the value of volunteers.

'Volunteering makes such a difference to new arrivals to Australia. As well as helping people learn English, it gives them connections into the community and helps them navigate what can be an unfamiliar new society,' she said. 'We find that the volunteers themselves also get a lot out of these relationships.'

CHAPTER 19
REFUGEE MUSICIAN REACHES OUT ACROSS THE GLOBE

The latest 'craze' among the hundreds of thousands of people who make up the global Karen diaspora is a young man who lives on Melbourne's western outskirts and spends much of his time volunteering in a local garden.

But 22-year-old Hba Hae's first passion is music and his latest homemade pop videos have just racked up one million YouTube hits. Under the stage name 'Star Boy' Hba has become an idol to young Karen in communities and refugee camps across the globe. Using a borrowed camera, he has filmed, performed, directed and edited a string of clips of his own songs, which have gone viral online and given him a following that extends to Karen communities in the US, UK, Malaysia, Holland, Sweden, Australia as well as in the camps along the Thai border.

Hba grew up in one of these camps where his parents fled when civil war came to their village in Burma. The Burmese Government has persecuted the Karen hill-tribe people since 1949 and there are an estimated 150,000 Karen living in the camps.

He spent most of his life in the teeming Mae La refugee camp among 50,000 other displaced Karen before coming to Australia as a refugee in September 2013.

'Life was tough in the camp,' Hba said, speaking through an interpreter. 'In summer there was not enough water and sometimes not enough food. We went to school but we could not leave the camp.'

Hba says music was an escape for him during these difficult times and he often entertained his fellow Karen with his music.

'When I wrote a sad song — maybe about losing someone — it sort of reflected the sadness of the Karen people. But when I wrote a happy song, it made people happy and maybe they would forget their problems for a time,' he said.

But it is only since coming to Australia that Hba can see an opportunity to follow his dream of a career in music.

'A few years ago in the camp there was no chance to have a band or make music properly. We had no money and no equipment. I had to play and sing by myself,' Hba said. 'Now in Australia I have more chance to play music and to start working towards my dream of playing music full time.'

Hba says he started singing and writing music in the camp when he was 16.

'I was listening to the local radio stations and to all sorts of music and I started writing and singing my own music,' he said. 'Music is very important to me and I want to improve my singing. I go to sleep each night singing and thinking about music and wake up each morning the same. When I get a free day I just want to sing and write music.'

And like almost every other Australian musician, Hba wants to crack the American market.

'I hope to become more popular as a Karen singer and I hope to become famous with Karen people living in the US and across the world as well as in the camps, where I came from,' he said.

Hba also recognises the influence he has on other young Karen, many of whom are marginalised and vulnerable.

'I also want to be a good person; a good example to other young Karen people,' he said.

Hba says he finds his inspiration where most other young songwriters do; in love and loss, family and art. But he also writes songs about his people's troubles.

'It is important to me to write about what is happening in Burma and what is happening to the Karen people,' Hba said.

Living with his parents, three brothers and two sisters in Hoppers Crossing, west of Melbourne, Hba is studying to improve his English and doing volunteer work in the gardens at Werribee Park. Werribee Park's Chief Ranger James Brincat says Hba is a superstar in the making.

'Hba is known to Karen people across the globe and his music is obviously very popular,' James said. 'It's amazing to think a million people have watched his latest video clip — filmed here at Werribee Park — yet here he is weeding and digging in the garden and living in very humble circumstances in the local community. Hba's story sums up the Karen people. They are such generous, gentle people who value family, friendship and music.'

Syrian refugee 'George' survived a year as a captive of ISIS; treated brutally, constantly threatened with death and not knowing the fate of his wife and daughter (chapter 1).

Rohingya refugees from Burma now living in Melbourne and collecting clothes to send to their countrymen who have sought refuge in Bangladesh. Abdul Majid on the right (chapter 2).

Somali refugee Hamdi Ubeed lost contact with her biological family for almost a decade. Determined to find them, she was finally reunited with her mother and brothers now living in a refugee camp in Kenya (chapter 4).

After spending years in a camp on the Thai-Burma border, Karen-Burmese refugee Evelyn Kunoo has become a leader in her community, inspiring many of them to find opportunities for work and study (chapter 6).

Forced to flee Syria's brutal Assad regime, Akram Abouhamdan and his wife Joumana have opened the first Syrian food shop in Carlton's Lygon Street (chapter 3).

Syrian farmer Danial Haron fought alongside Australian troops during WWII. But when, in May 2015, ISIS destroyed his village, the 93-year-old was forced to flee leaving behind his life's work (chapter 7).

As a small boy sitting on his father's shoulders, Hap Dan escaped Cambodia's infamous killing fields. Always grateful for his parents' sacrifices, Hap has built a new life for himself in Australia (chapter 8).

Antoun Gharibeh, his wife Noor and their three children saw everything they had worked towards shattered in just a few short months when war came to Syria. On their journey to safety in Australia, they overcame gun battles, breast cancer and near destitution (chapter 9).

After fleeing war in her native Eritrea, Nadia Hassan has raised family and built a thriving import and retail business in the heart of multicultural Footscray, in Melbourne's west (chapter 10).

Afghan refugee Elnaz Tavancheh's determination to get an education saw her defy 147 years of tradition to become the first female to attend Melbourne's prestigious Catholic all-boys school Parade College (chapter 20).

Karen refugee Hba Hae's passion is music. Under the stage name 'Star Boy', his home-made pop videos have racked up more than a million YouTube hits (chapter 19).

Iranian forensic scientist Nik Salehi was brutally tortured when he refused to fake drug reports implicating political dissidents in drugs crimes carrying the death penalty. After fleeing his homeland, he is trying to rebuild his life in Australia (chapter 21).

When Afghan bookbinder and printer 'Amini' published a version of the Qur'an in his native language it triggered a six year journey that saw him on the run from the Taliban and dodging death sentences imposed by conservative Islamic clerics (chapter 24).

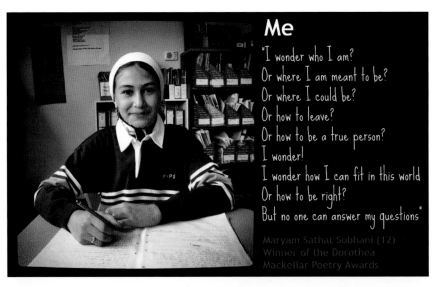

Me

"I wonder who I am?
Or where I am meant to be?
Or where I could be?
Or how to leave?
Or how to be a true person?
I wonder!
I wonder how I can fit in this world
Or how to be right?
But no one can answer my questions"

Maryam Sathat Sobhani (12)
Winner of the Dorothea
Mackellar Poetry Awards

Just two years after arriving in Australia and encountering the English language for the first time, 12-year-old Iranian refugee Maryam Sathat Sobhani won a prestigious national poetry prize (chapter 22).

Playing the music he loved put Iranian saxophonist Hadi Mohammadi in an impossible position; either give up his dream of carving a career and a life out of music or risk ending up in jail or worse. Hadi chose a third option – to leave his homeland and follow his dream (chapter 23).

Dandenong, in Melbourne's south east, has become a beacon for Afghan Hazaras who have fled decades long persecution and genocide in their homeland in southern Afghanistan (chapter 26).

Winning the *Afghan Idol* TV talent quest was both a blessing and burden for Afghan refugee Navid Forogh – it launched his music career but also brought him to the attention of the Taliban (chapter 29).

CHAPTER 20
FROM PERSIA TO PARADE COLLEGE – AN UNLIKELY REFUGEE JOURNEY

It was one of those unlikely stories that restores faith in human nature when an asylum seeker defied 147 years of tradition to become the first female to attend the prestigious Catholic all-boys school, Parade College.

Elnaz Tavancheh, an ethnic Hazara who fled her home in Iran to avoid persecution and threats, completed her VCE at the school in 2017 and is hoping to study at university.

After fleeing to Indonesia from Iran and taking a dangerous boat journey to Christmas Island, she and her mother are now living in Melbourne's northern suburbs.

She gained a place at Parade College through connections she made while in asylum detention and says the experience has been 'fun and exciting'.

'I was scared on the very first day — everyone was much taller than me. But all of the boys were very welcoming and very respectful. The teachers and the principal were great and I really enjoyed being part of the school,' Elnaz said.

She said the school was a little worried at first and told her they could not be sure how the boys would react to her.

'For the first week it was bit uncomfortable with everyone looking at me. I was a little afraid,' Elnaz said. 'But I wore the school uniform to try to blend in and after a little while the boys all accepted me as a fellow student and a friend.'

There was also concern about how Elnaz would handle being among 1,800 boys.

'I told them that on the boat I was among 50 single men and in detention I was among 200 single men,' she said.

Elnaz's presence at the school also served to educate some of the boys on issues around asylum seekers and refugees.

'My best friend at school didn't know anything about asylum seekers before he met me. He told me that his parents were against refugees coming to Australia but that when they met me and realised that I was just another human being, it changed their minds,' she said.

Elnaz arrived on Christmas Island on 12 March 2013 — her birthday — after a boat journey from Indonesia.

'When the navy found us, they asked our dates of birth. When I said March 12, the lady said: "that's today, happy birthday, you are gifted a new life on your birthday".'

Elnaz had just completed a year and a half of agricultural science studies at university when her family was reported to the government as illegal residents.

An Afghan Hazara, she had lived all of her life as a second-generation refugee in Iran. For decades, the Hazara, an ethnic minority from Afghanistan, have been oppressed, banned from educational opportunities and professional or government jobs. Hundreds of thousands have fled Afghanistan from other countries including Pakistan and Iran.

As mostly Shia Muslims, they have been targets of violence by extremist Sunni Muslim groups such as the Taliban and Lashkar-e-Jhangri. More than 1,500 have been killed and 4,000 maimed over the past decade in Pakistan and not a single perpetrator has been brought to justice in that time. It is not known how many more have been killed by the Taliban inside Afghanistan.

'Life became very difficult for us in Iran — my parents came to Iran when they were very young and they met and married there,' Elnaz said. 'At that time, you could live a reasonably comfortable life in Iran if you were a refugee. You could get a fake ID card which meant your children could go to school and you could live normally. But after the revolution things got worse for us Hazara. We knew many people who were caught with fake ID cards and sent back to Afghanistan. One of my cousins was sent back. He was caught by the Taliban and they cut off his fingers and took all his money. So, we were very afraid of being sent back to Afghanistan. Lots of families were sent back despite their children having been born in Iran.'

With personal threats being made against them and the prospect of being sent to strife-torn Afghanistan, Elnaz and her mother felt they had no option but to flee.

'We could not go back to Afghanistan because of the dangers there and it was impossible to stay in Iran,' she said.

Elnaz's father died when she was four from injuries he received fighting at the front in the Iran-Iraq war.

'My dad's lungs were damaged by chemical weapons in the war and he was in hospital for months,' she said.

Even though he had fought for the country for eight years, the Iranian authorities refused him a pension or any support after the war because he was an ethnic Hazara.

'He had no money, no pension and my mother and five kids to support so he went away to another city to work in construction. But that winter was particularly cold and he caught pneumonia. He was in hospital for three months before he passed away,' she said.

Elnaz's path to Parade College began while she was still inside the Melbourne Immigration Transit Accommodation centre in Broadmeadows.

'There was a lady called Caterina who came to visit asylum seekers who I got to know. When I got my bridging visa and was released, she invited me to work as a volunteer at her kinder. I was asked to speak to a group of Christian Brothers about my experiences. There I met Mark O'Laughlin, one of the brothers and a scientist at Melbourne Museum. Mark has been very good to me. He invited me to work with him at the museum in the marine biology lab. He gave me a microscope to work with and he even named a new species of sea cucumber he discovered after me: *Globosita Elnazae*.'

Parade College is supported by the Christian Brothers and Mr O'Laughlin arranged for Elnaz to attend the school. She completed her VCE, studying Physics, Chemistry, Maths Methods, Biology, English and

Persian. As an asylum seeker on a bridging visa, Elnaz does not have the right to publicly funded education and she cannot afford the $40,000 fee for a science degree at Melbourne University. She's hoping to get a scholarship to do nursing or agricultural science. In the meantime, she is volunteering at the Melbourne Museum.

'The main thing for myself and my mother is that we are safe now — and we are grateful for that,' Elnaz said. 'But I hope I can continue to study. I don't want to sit at home. And I hope that I can stay in Australia and have a future and a career. I would dearly love to give something back to the country that has given my mother and myself safety and a refuge from everything we feared back home.'

CHAPTER 21
STANDING UP FOR TRUTH IN THE FACE OF TORTURE – A VICTIM'S STORY

Arrested four times, brutally tortured and his career in ruins — Iranian asylum seeker Nik Salehi is hoping he can rebuild his life in Australia.

Although he is happy to be safe from the clutches of the Iranian intelligence service, his future is uncertain and he is not sure whether he will be allowed to stay in Australia or when he will see his family again. He is being treated for depression and post-traumatic stress and has not seen his wife and son in almost two years.

Nik, an ethnic Arab, was a medical scientist and university official until he fell foul of Iran's notorious intelligence service. After graduating from his university medical studies, he did compulsory military service and then returned to his home city of Shadeghan, which has a largely Arab population. He held a senior position in a forensic drug laboratory working on testing samples from people accused of drug offences. Around this time a group of dissidents in Shadeghan began protesting against the government of Mahmoud Ahmadinejad over the denial of rights to Arab citizens in Iran.

'A lot of people were not happy with the government. They protested against the government and a group of prominent dissidents emerged saying they would fight for the ordinary people,' Nik said.

He was approached by agents of the Iranian intelligence service who demanded he produce fake drug reports implicating some of the leading dissidents in drugs crimes.

'They wanted me to help them manufacture drug cases against these people. My problems all started from here. Having just seven grams of certain drugs means a death penalty in Iran,' Nik said. 'I had many people supporting me, saying I should not agree to do this so I refused.

Some of the people they wanted me to implicate were my friends. So, because I took a stand against what they wanted from me, they made a case against me.'

Nik was arrested at work and taken to a prison where he was put in a small dark room.

'I was in the room for 11 days — not knowing exactly where I was or what time of day it was,' he said. 'This was where the torture started. I was released on condition that I cooperate with them — but still my friends said not to.'

Nik was arrested for a second time and jailed for six months after being convicted of anti-government activities.

'I was placed in the small room again — this time for about 15 days. They tortured me physically, mentally and emotionally,' he said.

Nik finds it painful to recount his torture ordeal and was visibly upset when he did. But he said he wanted people to know what had happened to him. He described how his ankles were bound and he was hung from the ceiling for hours. He was 'waterboarded', which means he was bound to a chair and had a cloth placed over his mouth and nose. Cold water was then poured over the cloth making it difficult to breathe. This form of torture can cause an individual to experience the sensation of drowning. It can cause extreme pain, dry drowning, damage to lungs, brain damage from oxygen deprivation, broken bones due to struggling against restraints and lasting psychological damage. Nik says he was also stripped and sexually assaulted. He had a steel bowl placed over his head which was then hit repeatedly with a hammer — causing painful sounds and vibrations. He said that the easiest part of his nightmare to endure was being thrown in a corner and punched and kicked.

'The worst thing,' he said, 'was when they told me they had my wife and were going to sexually abuse her or kill her. That was the worst kind of mental torture.'

After his release, Nik moved to another city called Ahvaz to work.

'I thought that maybe they would forget about me, but I was wrong,' he said. 'There were protests during the election of Amadinejad and I was a supporter of the reformist candidate Mir Hossein Mousavi. My name appeared on a list of Mousavi supporters that was seized by the intelligence service. I was locked up in the small room for a third time and tortured again for about 10 to 15 days. After that I left Iran. My friends told me I had better leave the country. So I went to Indonesia and boarded a boat to Australia and arrived here on 28 August 2012.'

Nik is being treated by a psychologist for the effects of torture.

'What happened still affects me severely, I can't sleep and I can't concentrate on things,' he said.

When Nik left Iran, his son was 15 months old — he is now seven.

'I have not seen my son since he was a baby. My wife is raising him alone and she is also seeing a doctor and taking medicine because of what happened to us,' he said.

Nik says he is slowly recovering from his ordeal. Recently, he phoned his wife and says he is feeling better for it. But he says he keeps his once-every-two-months calls short for fear of retribution and because he knows the lines are tapped.

Nik is also volunteering at a local church and says he has been exploring a long-held interest in Buddhism.

CHAPTER 22
ASYLUM SEEKER WINS NATIONAL POETRY PRIZE

Twelve-year-old Maryam Sathat Sobhani had only been in Australia for a year and first encountered the English language just two years before winning a national poetry prize.

The daughter of asylum seekers from Iran, Maryam wrote a poem titled *Me* which won the Upper Primary category in the 2014 Dorothea Mackellar Poetry Awards, the oldest and largest poetry competition for school-aged children in Australia. The awards celebrate the work of Australian poet and writer Dorothea Mackellar, the author of the iconic Australian poem *My Country*. Maryam's poem alludes to the uncertainties of life and a sense of self for people who are displaced from their traditional homes.

She and her family travelled to Gunnedah, in NSW, for the awards ceremony.

'I like to write, I like to talk about my feelings,' said Maryam, who is now in Year 10.

Her teacher at North Footscray Primary School, in Melbourne's west, Thomas Hortop said Maryam is a bright child who drives herself to try new things. 'She's a smart kid and she's very competitive. She throws herself into all of the sports we have in our PE program and she is very keen to learn,' he said. 'Her English has come on very well in such a short time and she works hard to improve it.'

Mr Hortop said children at the school had been encouraged to write a few poems to enter in the awards. 'Maryam wrote 38 poems,' he said, 'it shows how driven she is to try her very best.'

Maryam and her family hail from Shiraz, in western Iran, which is known as a city of poets and literature and was the home of the famous

Persian poets Hafiz, Saadi and Rumi — whose work Mathnawi is one of the literary glories of the Middle-East.

Despite her success with words, Maryam says maths is her favourite subject.

Maryam and her family fled Iran in 2012. Her father ran a pizza restaurant and ice cream shop but the Iranian authorities closed it because of its associations with the West and its function as a gathering place for young people.

'The police came and sprayed everyone with pepper spray. They made us close the shop and warned us that we would go to jail,' Mr Sobhani said.

The family left Iran and came by boat to Australia from Indonesia. They spent time on Manus Island, on Christmas Island and in detention in Darwin before being released in Melbourne.

'Life in Iran became very hard for us with the government. But here things are much better and Maryam can go to a good school. She was not treated well at school in Iran. Now we hope she will have opportunities,' Mr Sobhani said.

Maryam's winning poem

Me

I wonder who I am?
Or where I am meant to be?
Or where I could be?
Or how to leave?
Or how to be a true person?
I wonder!
I wonder how I can fit in this world
Or how to be right?
But no one can answer my questions.

CHAPTER 23
A MUSICIAN'S BATTLE TO BE HEARD

Playing the music he loves put Iranian saxophonist Hadi Mohammadi in an invidious position. Either give up his dream of carving a career and a life out of music or risk ending up in jail — or worse.

The crackdown on secular music by the authorities in his homeland — and the fact that he had been arrested and locked up several times — left Hadi no choice but to gather his family and flee.

Hadi and his wife and child caught a plane to Indonesia and found a people smuggler to take them to Australia by boat.

'I could not stay in Iran after the government cracked down on musicians. The only places we could play were in underground venues — sometimes literally in cellars,' Hadi said. 'I am a musician — it is all I know how to do. Once I had been arrested a couple of times I was a marked man for the government. I knew they might come for me at any time.' If I wanted to live — if I wanted a life, I had to leave,' said Hadi, who studied the saxophone in the UK.

He said the boat journey was a 13-day ordeal with rough weather and sickness among the passengers.

'It was very bad and I was afraid for my family but I didn't have any choice if I wanted to have a safe life and live my dream to play music,' Hadi said.

Since the establishment of the Islamic Republic of Iran, music has been the subject of fierce political and religious debate. Its legal and social status has constantly been changing and continues to be the object of various restrictions because of music's purported power to seduce and corrupt.

From early on, the official position of the Islamic regime was unmistakable. All concerts, and especially all radio and television broadcasts of foreign and Iranian, classical and popular music, were banned. The only genres of music acceptable in the Iranian republic are Iranian folk music; Iranian classical or 'traditional' music and a heavily censored form of pop music that is almost universally unpopular with young people.

Under these strict rules however, an underground music culture has flourished. The very intention of abolishing music in public life has unexpectedly led to the practice of music groups forming within family circles or among people of the younger generation of all social classes.

In January 2013, five Tehran musicians were arrested and jailed on charges of collaborating with LA-based musicians and satellite channels. The police raid was apparently prompted by the recording and distribution of a song with political content that the regime found objectionable.

'In Iran there are rules about everything. If you want to play or record music, you have to get permission but there is a lot of corruption so it's not that easy,' Hadi said. 'Even if you think you have got permission, the government can come along and stop you and lock you up and even accuse you of terrible things like being a traitor, being an infidel.'

Since arriving in Australia, Hadi has been playing with a number of bands. As an asylum seeker on a bridging visa, he does not have work rights, but plays as a volunteer. He is involved with groups playing classical music, swing, big band and blues — music he could never hope to perform publicly in Iran.

'In Australia there is freedom to play whatever music you like. I am playing with three very good groups and I feel very good about this,' Hadi said. 'Here people appreciate many kinds of music and I hope I can work as a musician one day.'

CHAPTER 24
SIX YEARS ON THE RUN FROM THE BOOK BURNERS

When Afghan bookbinder and printer Amini published a version of the Qur'an in his native language it triggered a six-year saga that has seen him on the run from the Taliban and dodging death sentences imposed by conservative Islamic clerics administering relentless, inflexible and sometimes brutal Sharia law.

He spent years in hiding in Iran, Indonesia and Malaysia — constantly looking over his shoulder for the agents of militant fundamentalist Islam.

Amini and his business partners became so infamous in Afghanistan that they were forced to use false names and keep their heads down for fear of being identified and outed as 'infidels' deserving of death.

Finally, he boarded an asylum seeker boat bound for Australia. Now he says he feels safe for the first time in years and can sleep without nightmares.

'I was one of a group of five people running a company that produced books. We translated books from other languages like Russian, Spanish and Hindi — mostly for kids,' Amini said. 'We would translate them, print them and send them to the market. One day we decided to produce a copy of the Qur'an in local languages including Dari — it was a big mistake.'

At the behest of influential conservative clerics, who maintain that the Qur'an can only be read in the original Arabic, the Afghan Government sued the men and shut down their printing company. Not to be outdone, the Taliban put a $US5 million bounty on the heads of the five men who were forced to flee.

'It was a bad experience. It was frightening. People wrote on the walls of our homes that we were "animals" and we were worthless,' Amini said. 'All we wanted to do was to give people copies of a Qur'an they could read in their own language — most Afghans, and especially the kids, cannot read Arabic. We could not go back to our homes — it was too dangerous. That's why we ran away — to save our lives.'

Amini took refuge in Iran for several years but his status there was tenuous.

'If the Iranian authorities had known about us they would have locked us up or sent us back to Afghanistan,' he said.

Leaving his home and his family in Afghanistan was the start of six years on the run for Amini.

'I was always looking over my shoulder in Iran and even in Malaysia and Indonesia — which are both Islamic countries. I was frightened someone might recognise me and then the militants would come after me.'

Amini's final journey to Australia was not without its challenges. He and 14 other Afghan asylum seekers spent 24 hours baling water out of their sinking boat before they were rescued by the Royal Australian Navy.

'The water was up to our chests and some people had given up hope. We thought we were going to die,' he said.

Amini says that since arriving in Australia he has been able to sleep properly for the first time.

'I feel safe here for the first time in years — my sleep is not interrupted with nightmares and I feel I can start to live again,' he said.

But for several years, Amini was on a bridging visa and had no work rights.

'I was just waiting. I had no idea what would happen.'

With time on his hands, Amini has also returned to his hobby of bodybuilding. He also found some solace as a member of an asylum seeker choir.

'When I came to the choir I can see some friends and meet new people. It's very nice to be with other people and to share some singing and some cooking,' Amini said. 'The best thing is when we go on stage. We performed in front of 1,500 people. That was amazing. That was fantastic.'

Amini saw his mother recently for the first time in years, meeting at a location in South East Asia.

'She gave me a hug and I realised that your mother is the best thing in your life. We should all appreciate what they do for us,' he said.

Amini has recently been granted work rights and is working as a labourer.

There is no published law in Afghanistan prohibiting the translation of the Qur'an. But Amini was accused of violating Islamic Shariah law by modifying the Qur'an. The courts in Afghanistan, an Islamic state, are empowered to apply Shariah law when there are no applicable existing statutes. And Afghanistan's court system appears to be stacked against those accused of religious crimes. Judges don't want to seem soft on potential heretics and lawyers don't want to be seen defending them, according to Afzal Shurmach Nooristani, whose Afghan Legal Aid group defends people accused of religious offences. Mr Nooristani says he and his colleagues have received death threats.

'The mullahs in the mosques have said whoever defends an infidel is an infidel,' he said.

Sentences on religious infractions can be harsh. In January 2008, a court sentenced a journalism student to death for blasphemy for asking questions about women's rights under Islam. An appeals court reduced the sentence to 20 years in prison. In 2006, an Afghan man was sentenced to death for converting to Christianity. He was later ruled insane and was given asylum in Italy. Islamic leaders and the parliament accused President Hamid Karzai of being a puppet for the West for letting him live.

Shariah law is applied differently in Islamic states. Saudi Arabia claims the Qur'an as its constitution, while Malaysia has separate religious and secular courts. But since there is no ultimate arbiter of religious questions in Afghanistan, judges must strike a balance between the country's laws and proclamations by clerics or the Islamic council, called the Ulema council.

Mr Nooristani says that judges are so nervous about annoying the Ulema council and being criticised that they tend to push the Islamic cases aside and just defer to what others say. Deferring to the council means that edicts issued by the group of clerics can influence rulings more than laws on the books or a judge's own interpretation of Shariah law. Judges have to be careful about whom they might anger with their rulings. In September 2008, gunmen killed a top judge with Afghanistan's counter-narcotics court in the latest of a string of judicial assassinations.

CHAPTER 25
ONE WOMAN'S REFUGEE JOURNEY

Melika Yassin Sheikh-Eldin is one of Australia's great refugee success stories.

After fleeing war in Eritrea in the late 1970s she completed a doctorate, set up refugee-centred social enterprises and helped thousands of new arrivals to Australia settle successfully.

Melika has been instrumental in developing world-leading settlement programs and represented AMES and Australia at United Nations forums.

She was a key player in the successful establishment of a Burmese Karen community at Nhill, in western Victoria and played a major role in an initiative to engage local Karen women as volunteers in the gardens at Werribee Park — which has gone a long way to alleviating issues of isolation and mental health and wellbeing among the large Karen community in Werribee. The community garden model is now being adopted by other organisations.

As part of the Horn of Africa Communities Network, Melika also helped a large South Sudanese community settle in Warrnambool and other groups settle in Swan Hill, Mildura and Shepparton.

Since 2007, she has sat on the board of the Refugee Council of Australia and has been a 'Refugee Voice' at the annual UNHCR consultations in Geneva.

Currently, Melika is AMES' Manager of International and Community Development. She found it difficult to find work in her chosen area of Marine Biology but along her journey as a refugee she found a passion for work in the humanitarian sector. Melika has been working for AMES since 2001.

'Originally, I came from Eritrea. I was brought up in a middle-class family in an agricultural town,' Melika said. 'I had completed first year university studies in medicine when the war came and that changed everything for me.'

Full scale war came to Eritrea when the government in Ethiopia unilaterally revoked Eritrea's autonomous status. The war went on for 33 years until 1991 when the Eritrean People's Liberation Front (EPLF), having defeated the Ethiopian forces in Eritrea, took control of the country.

In April 1993, in a referendum supported by Ethiopia, the Eritrean people voted almost unanimously in favour of independence. Formal international recognition of an independent and sovereign Eritrea followed later the same year. But Eritrea's militarist government and continuing dispute with Ethiopia has spawned allegations of human rights violations and fuelled a continuing refugee exodus.

'Obviously we were aware of the revolution which was mostly in the countryside — but when the war spread all over Eritrea we were forced to flee. We had friends and relatives who were killed during the conflict. I spent two years in a refugee camp in Sudan helping as a volunteer — I worked with UNHCR, Human Appeal International, Save the Children and other aid organisations. I was given a scholarship and I wanted to study medicine — but that was open only to local Sudanese — so my second choice was Zoology specialising in Fisheries and I graduated from Khartoum University with first degree honours.'

Unable to work, Melika volunteered for national service with the Eritrean revolutionary forces.

'After that I was contacted by the UNHCR who asked me to teach in one of its Secondary schools in eastern Sudan — so I did that for two years,' she said.

Offered the opportunity to do some post graduate study, Melika went to Egypt and completed a Master's Degree in Marine Biology studying Red Sea native fish.

'At the time there was an influx of refugees into Egypt from Sudan, Somalia, Ethiopia and other places in the region so I volunteered for St Andrews Church welfare Centre as an interpreter while I was doing my Master's Degree,' she said.

With the political situations in Eritrea and most of the rest of the Horn of Africa, Melika applied to the UN for resettlement and was accepted with her three sons into Australia in 1992. Her husband remained in Eritrea with the revolution and joined them in Australia in 1995.

'I came to Melbourne and applied to do a PhD — which had always been my dream. I achieved that by completing my doctorate on native Australian fresh water fish at Deakin University, Warrnambool Campus and publishing four papers on endangered species,' she said.

Like many refugees and new arrivals to Australia, Melika struggled to find work in her chosen field.

'As a refugee, I had always realised the importance of networking. Like in many places around the world, it's not what you know but who you know which matters,' she said. 'So my first job in Australia was at AMES, working two days a week at the Footscray facility helping newly-arrived young people to find educational courses that matched their needs and helping to fill out forms and so on.'

Melika then moved into full time work with AMES' newly established Community Division and she was instrumental in setting up ground breaking refugee social enterprises, such as Sorghum Sisters Catering, which still operates out of a Carlton primary school.

In 2005 AMES launched its Settlement Division which would go on to help thousands of refugees and asylum seekers settle in Victoria.

'I worked as a Senior Coordinator in Settlement and that has led on to all sorts of other things,' she said.

Melika is responsible for AMES' Community Guides Program, training for staff, orientation for new arrivals and Community Engagement — a program which seeks to link people to their local communities and mitigate issues such as isolation and mental health and wellbeing.

It was under this role that Melika played part in establishing the Karen community at Nhill, in western Victoria, and also in engaging the Karen community at Wyndham to volunteer in the gardens at Werribee Park. The program to settle Karen-Burmese refugees at Nhill has emerged as a model not only for refugee settlement but also for the revival of struggling rural towns. About 150 Karen refugees have been settled in Nhill, attracted by jobs being offered by local poultry producer Luv-a-Duck. Local leaders say the arrival of the Karen has breathed new life into the town, bringing economic benefits and enriching its cultural life.

At Werribee and in partnership with Parks Victoria, a similar program has meant the regeneration of an historic garden and, in a remarkable example of cultural cross-pollination, the blossoming of local refugee communities. What started as a call for volunteers to help rebuild the gardens at Werribee turned into a therapy session for dislocated and isolated refugee families.

'It has also turned out to be an incredibly successful social experiment and a model for other community engagement projects,' Melika said. 'In partnership with Parks Victoria, we began the program as a way of engaging the older isolated women from the local Karen community by offering them the opportunity to come to the garden. But now the young people and men are coming — the whole community have embraced it and we have some young men studying horticulture as trainees with Parks Victoria.'

The Park's Chief Ranger James Brincat says: 'Everyone involved in this is blown away by what we've achieved and the inspirational outcomes that have come from putting some seeds in the ground and seeing what happens — both literally and figuratively. A lot of the credit should go to Melika.'

Melika says her work has become a passion. 'I have been honoured to represent AMES internationally as a world-leading settlement organisation,' she said.

Melika has travelled overseas, including to Sweden, New Zealand and Japan, to help other organisations establish community guide programs along the AMES model. The programs recruit former refugees with first language skills, and who have experienced displacement and resettlement, as guides to help newly arrived people navigate a new society and help with the practical necessities of life.

'I'm passionate about identifying needs and developing programs to help the resettlement of refugees,' Melika said. 'With the Nhill project,

AMES first consulted with the communities to see if such a project addresses their needs — we planned the whole project and made sure there was direct community engagement and involvement — that was a key to its success. 'I'm also big on partnerships — in my language we say: "one hand cannot clap but many hands clap loudly".'

CHAPTER 26
LOOKING FOR A PROMISED LAND – THE HAZARAS OF DANDENONG

Walk into the Bestway Supermarket on Dandenong's Lonsdale Street and you'll immediately see 20 litre cans of sunflower oil and 80 litre cooking pots stacked neatly near the entrance. There are also posters advertising Qur'an classes, English lessons and home child care. This simple social accoutrement gives you an oblique insight into Dandenong's close-knit Afghan Hazara community.

Bestway's co-owner Mohammad Reza says: 'Australians come in and see the big pots and they laugh. But what they don't realise is that if we have a get-together or a party at someone's house — and we Hazara have lots of these functions — there will be 60 or 70 people and they all have to be fed.'

Reza was one of the first Hazaras to settle in Dandenong in the late 1990s. He worked for three years in a slaughterhouse in Pakenham and then opened a small shop on Thomas Street, one block back from the main drag. He sold groceries and other items to an almost exclusive Afghan and Iranian clientele.

In January 2014, Reza and his brother and a cousin opened the Bestway Supermarket on a prime spot in central Dandenong opposite the imposing, recently refurbished Drum Theatre. The tidy, well-stocked shop serves as many locals as it does Afghans; you can buy Vegemite and Tim Tams as well as sheep's brains and Lavash bread.

The Hazara community around Dandenong has grown steadily over the past fifteen-or-so years to the point where there are now an estimated 12,000 living in the area which now extends to Narre Warren, Hampton Park and Cranbourne.

The first Hazaras arrived in the late 1990s as attacks on them in

Afghanistan and in the Pakistani city of Quetta, to which many had fled from the Taliban, increased exponentially.

As mostly Shia Muslims, the Hazara are targets for violence by extremist Sunni Muslim groups such as the Taliban and Lashkar-e-Jhangri. More than 1,500 have been killed and 4,000 maimed over the past decade in Pakistan and not a single perpetrator has been brought to justice in that time. It is not known how many more have been killed by the Taliban inside Afghanistan.

Hazaras are the third largest ethnic group in Afghanistan, at about 2.8 million, the majority of whom are Shiite Muslims. They also have a population approaching 500,000 in neighbouring Pakistan.

The word Hazar means 'thousand' in Persian and some experts believe they are descendants of Mongol soldiers left by Genghis Khan in the 13th century; a theory supported by the Hazaras' distinctive Asiatic facial features. The Hazara comprise the largest ethnic group seeking asylum in Australia and this exodus from terror in Afghanistan and Pakistan has produced a two-tier community among the Hazara in Dandenong. There are those who have jobs or businesses and relatively settled and comfortable lives. And there are those who arrived after August 2013 — as Australian politics became consumed with the 'boat people' issue — who do not have work rights and whose futures are uncertain.

The asylum seekers without work rights are typically single men, sharing cheap housing and existing on benefits payments that are less than the dole. Despite this, the Hazaras have built a vibrant community and sub-economy in Melbourne's south-east.

Photographer Barat Ali Batoor, who has compiled a photo exhibition on the community, says the Hazara community is defined by its circumstances.

'It's a very close community because we are all a long way from home and we all know what is happening there — there have been so many Hazaras killed in the past few years and anyone who knows anything about the political situation in Pakistan and Afghanistan will tell you that it is only going to get worse,' he said.

Batoor, who worked as a photojournalist in Afghanistan and
whose exposure of the sex slave trade in his home country earned
him international recognition and made him a target for the Taliban
and conservative interests, says there are strong cultural bonds in the
Hazara community.

'Hazaras tend to look out for each other and they're very social. In
Dandenong there is a very strong Hazara cultural scene. There are youth
groups, music groups, theatre, sporting groups and other community
activities,' he said.

Mohammad Danesh runs a recycling business. He came to Australia
in 2005 as a refugee from Ghazani Province in Afghanistan sponsored
by family members already living here. Originally he settled in Sunshine
— at the time there were five or six Hazara families living there.

'We stayed about a year,' he said. 'Then we moved to Narre Warren
South — close to Dandenong — where the majority of Afghans live. It
was easier to communicate and connect with the community.'

Mohammad opened a supermarket and grocery business with some
partners. After two-and-a-half years he left to open a recycling business,
which is still running.

Mohammad's son Bashir runs a travel agency and money exchange
in a Dandenong arcade dominated by Afghan and other immigrant-run
businesses. Bashir was 13 when he arrived in Australia and completed
his VCE and went on to study international business and aviation.

'Language is one of the main issues for Afghans looking for work here.
So it's very important to learn English,' Bashir said. 'Because I was quite
young when I came to Australia it was easier for me.'

Bashir says there is a small Hazara-based economy running in the
Dandenong area which provides some employment for newly arrived
migrants and refugees.

'We have, for example, Hazara businesses which import things you
can't buy in Australian shops. This makes it easier for people in the
community to get their traditional goods and it gives some people jobs.'

Not far from Bashir's arcade lives a man who does not have a job
nor a business to run. 'Syed' fled his home in Quetta in fear of his life

— leaving behind his wife and children and his elderly mother. As a middle ranking public servant and a Hazara, he attracted the attention of the Taliban.

'I had to leave because there were men with guns looking for me. My colleagues at work told me not to come to work because these men had come to my office looking for me,' Syed said.

He arrived in Australia after August 2013 and so does not have the right to work. 'It is very difficult for us because we cannot work. We just sit at home with nothing much to do and with very little money,' he said.

Asylum seekers receive 89 per cent of Centrelink benefits — or just over $200 a week for a single adult. 'It is very hard. We want to work but we cannot. We would like to work to support ourselves and our families — we do not want to take money from the Australian Government,' Syed said.

Taiba Kiran, an Education Counsellor with refugee and migrant settlement agency AMES, and herself a Hazara, sees her own community from a range of perspectives. 'It's a very close-knit community and people are very helpful toward each other. People already here are established and working to help new arrivals to settle in,' she said.

Kiran says Dandenong became a magnet for the Hazara because a critical mass of population was achieved. 'You had a few Hazara living here and that attracted more and then more,' she said. 'There was also affordable and available housing and all the key services are here. The Hazara are just the most recent wave of immigration that Dandenong has seen over decades. You had the Greeks and Italian in the 1950s, then Albanians and Vietnamese — now its Afghans. Businesses were established here that provided the special requirements — halal meat and other food imported from Afghanistan or surrounding countries,' she said.

Another prominent Hazara woman is Zakia Baig. She founded the Australian Hazara Women's Friendship Network (AHWFN) in November 2012, with the aim of helping other Hazara women feel comfortable in Australia by providing them with a social network and building their confidence.

'Friendship is the main focus,' she said. 'We want them to feel welcome, accepted, and part of the broader Australian community.'

Her organisation gives women the opportunity to receive regular training as well as free English classes in their own language. They start by building basic skills, such as English, finding friends in the Dandenong community and gaining the knowledge and confidence to access services, use public transport and learn computer skills.

Zakia won SBS's *My Community Matters* competition in 2013 — by submitting a story outlining her journey from Pakistan to Australia, speaking about the importance of community and women's rights — and got the chance to share it with then Prime Minister Julia Gillard on Australia Day.

'We are working especially with newly arrived and older women who suffer isolation and a lack of connection with the broader community,' Zakia said. 'It is alarming for us because we can see that in the future our women might suffer even greater isolation. But we are meeting this challenge by taking them out and helping them mingle in the wider community. A lot of our women are not well educated or literate and this makes for a lot of communication problems. 'The cultural differences are also an issue. Many Afghans, and particularly women, have no understanding of other cultures and so no way of making friends from other cultures. 'One of our strengths though is that we are a close community and everyone tries to help one another — this is because we've been living in areas where discrimination and repression of Hazaras is very high.'

Zakia says Hazaras are different from most other ethnic groups in Afghanistan, Pakistan and Iraq.

'I think the Hazaras are more enterprising, more open and welcoming. They are secular, accepting and peaceful. Hazaras have the attitude that if you're going to survive, then you have to find a way to get on with people and make a life,' she said.

Zakia says the newly arrived Hazara asylum seekers who don't have work rights are accepted and included by more established members of the community but that the longer standing members could do more.

'Newly arrived people are included very much in community events but they still have their challenges,' she said. 'For instance the local community could do more to provide English classes for this group.' But overall, Zakia says the Hazara community is in good shape. 'I'm optimistic, as a community we are making progress. We have students going to uni — including young women — which would never happen in Afghanistan. More women are coming out of their homes and if they're given opportunities, they are very capable and keen to find ways to make contributions and to shine. These are very positive signs. Despite all the challenges we still face, Dandenong and Australia have been good for the Hazara.'

Bestway Supermarket owner Mohammad Reza is now an Australian citizen. He came here on an asylum seeker boat to escape the dangers he faced in his home city of Kabul.

'I am very happy to be here in Australia — not for myself but for my family. They are safe here and they have good lives,' he said. 'My son is studying civil engineering at uni and my daughter is in Year 11. They are both studying hard and want to be successful for themselves and also to help our community. I'm proud of my son and I dream sometimes that he will go back to Afghanistan one day as an engineer and help rebuild the country. My daughter wants to be a scientist and that is something we couldn't dream of in Afghanistan. They would never let us do these things because we are Hazara.'

Reza says many members of the Hazara community have family back home they worry about. 'I remember when I first came here, I would drive my car to a quiet place and cry because I felt bad about being away from my family,' he said. 'I'd love to go back to my country and take my children to show them how people live there — I consider my homeland like my mother. But unfortunately, the people there won't let me go back.'

Reza said Hazara people gravitated to Dandenong after a fledgling community was established.

'The immigration department put us all over the place so we had to find each other. We needed to help each other with learning English, finding work, schooling and even being able to shop for the things we needed. Also, all the facilities were located here — immigration, Centrelink and doctors and a lot of people don't have cars so they have to walk. Here in Dandenong it's easy for us to connect with each other and community is very important to us Hazaras. Hazaras are very social; we are accepting and we can get on with anyone. We get together a lot in big groups — that's why we need the big pots,' Reza laughs.

CHAPTER 27
CAPTURING DIVERSITY THROUGH A CAMERA LENS

A ground-breaking photographic project to capture the rich cultural diversity of Australia's public housing estates has been launched in Melbourne.

Photographer Abdullahi Ibrahim and a collaborator have begun photographing people living in public housing — starting in suburban Carlton, where they grew up.

'We want to try to capture the essence of the commission flats and government housing. Not many people have experienced what it's like to live in public housing,' Abdullahi said. 'We plan to go around Australia taking interesting photographs that will tell a story. For me, partly, it's an exercise in nostalgia because I grew up in public housing and I've always valued the sense of community where I lived and the amazing diversity. Everyone has a story about how they got there and I want to develop a narrative around that idea.'

He said that Australia had a very rich history of public housing and the onset of gentrification in inner city areas could see that history and cultural richness lost.

The Housing Commission of Victoria was established by the Housing Act of 1937 in response to slum housing in Melbourne and worked under the Slum Reclamation and Housing Act 1938. The mission was 'slum abolition' driven by the zeal of social reformers, but later became referred to as 'slum clearance' and 'block demolition'.

The Commission presided over the construction of the Melbourne Olympic Village in 1956, and made its mark on the Melbourne skyline during the 1960s in the form of high-rise blocks of flats on various sites

around inner Melbourne, the largest of which were in Lygon Street in
Carlton and Atherton Gardens in Fitzroy.

Approximately twenty of these precast concrete 20 to 30 storey
height buildings were constructed around Melbourne, until the type of
development fell into disrepute, mainly for sociological reasons. By 1970
nearly 4,000 privately owned dwellings had been compulsorily acquired
and replaced by nearly 7,000 high rise flats.

'We want to capture the rawness and the essence of these places before
it's too late. It's about capturing images of real people and telling their
stories. It's also about letting people tell their own stories through the
images,' Abdullahi said. 'The plan is to go to different commission flats
and capture different angles and local stories — and we're not sugar-
coating this, we understand the issues that exist in some of these places.'

After fleeing the civil war in his home town of Mogadishu, Somalia,
in 1991, Abdullahi and his family spent years in refugee camps in Kenya
and Yemen. He came to Australia aged five as a refugee in 1995 with
his mother, elder brother and twin sister. The family settled in housing
commission flats on Rathdowne Street in Carlton.

Abdullahi attended the local primary school and Northcote High
and is now in his final year studying chemical engineering at RMIT
University. But photography is his passion and something he would
like to eventually take up professionally. Abdullahi was a finalist in the
AMES/MAV 2013 Heartlands Refugee Art Prize with a photograph
titled 'Here!' depicting family members in a small boat.

'Photography started as a hobby for me and through a kind of organic
process it gradually developed into something more — it's a way of
experimenting and expressing myself,' Abdullahi said. 'I heard about
the Heartlands competition and at the time I was interested in images
around my environment so I thought I would enter one. The image
shows a boat built by a local community group — a replica of a native
American boat — and some of my family members.'

Abdullahi volunteers as a youth counsellor at the community group
Drummond Street Services and the boat was built over a year as one of
the organisation's youth projects.

'The boat project was designed to engage local kids and teach them some skills,' he said. 'The boat image tells a story and ultimately that is what interests me about photography — the opportunity to tell stories that transcend language and culture.'

CHAPTER 28
THE KAREN OF NHILL: AN EXPERIMENT IN REGIONAL SETTLEMENT

A program to settle Karen-Burmese refugees at Nhill, in western Victoria, is emerging as a model not only for refugee settlement but also for the revival of struggling rural towns. About 150 Karen refugees have been settled in Nhill, attracted by jobs being offered by local poultry producer Luv-a-Duck.

Local leaders say the arrival of the Karen has breathed new life into the town, bringing economic benefits and enriching its cultural life.

Hal Loo is emblematic of the Karen experience in Nhill. The 25-year-old apprentice mechanic at the local Halfway Motors loves his job and his community. 'I love coming to work and I love to go fishing,' he says. 'Nhill is a good place for us Karen.'

Hal, his parents, two brothers and three sisters spent years living in a tent in a United Nations refugee camp on the Thai-Burma border after the Burmese government burnt his village. The Burmese Government has persecuted the Karen hill-tribe people since 1949 and there are an estimated 150,000 Karen living in camps.

Hal came to the town, about 350 kilometres west of Melbourne, when his parents moved to the area to work for Luv-a-Duck. 'Coming here gave me the opportunity to see my dream of working with cars and machines come true,' Hal said. For all of the Karen of Nhill, it has been an incredible and unlikely journey from the rain-drenched jungles of South-East Asia to the broad wheat fields and silos of the Wimmera.

LOCAL HEROES

The settlement program was effectively begun by John Millington OAM, who in 2009 was General Manager of Luv-a-Duck.

With a lack of local labour to facilitate the company's expansion, Mr Millington turned to settlement agency AMES to see whether there were any refugees willing to relocate to Nhill. After arranging for a group of Karen to visit the Luv-a-Duck plant and Nhill, four workers were hired.

Now there are more than 50 Karen working at the plant and on local farms servicing it. 'We learnt very quickly that it was important that the partners and kids of the workers were involved. We knew that they had to be looked after, engaged and connected to the community or the whole thing would fall over,' Mr Millington said.

'You can't have the wife sitting at home not knowing anyone and it's the same with the kids. You just have to put them in touch with people and away they go,' he said. As Mr Millington learned more about the Karen and their plight, bringing them to Nhill became more than just a business initiative.

'For me learning about the Karen was a light bulb moment. I thought I must find out more about these people. I googled them and put together their story,' he said. 'The Karen needed some help and given their nature and the terrible experiences they had endured, I thought they might be a good fit for the community at Nhill.'

There were, however, cultural obstacles to overcome, including a fear of persecution by the authorities.

'I had showed them a map of where Nhill was and I told them it was "near the border" — meaning the border with South Australia. They were worried because they thought I meant the Thai border,' Mr Millington said. 'We took them on a bus tour around town. We stopped at the police station and on gets the local rural cop. There was silence and then the police sergeant smiled and said "hello" and you could hear the sighs of relief. We were worried about what the locals would think about us bringing a group of Asians to town so we brought all the community leaders together as well as the police, the mayor and the local priests. Initially, we took on four workers at Luv-a-Duck and we made sure they were good representatives of their community. Then they asked "can we bring another friend?" and it went from there.'

Mr Millington said that having local people champion the Karen was vital to the program's success.

'One of the key things that made the whole thing work was that the woman who lived directly opposite the house where we initially house the Karen was incredibly welcoming — she is a wonderfully caring person,' he said. 'I went to see her and told her I needed a grandma for the Karen and she responded. It was important because she is a person who knows everyone and everything that goes on in town. She was just wonderful and one of the main reasons the thing succeeded in the early days — she was someone looking out for the Karen on a daily basis,' Mr Millington said. He also spoke to Luv-a-Duck staff, explaining who the Karen were and where they had come from while giving assurances that the Karen would only get jobs that could not be filled by locals. 'We had no problems, no bad blood. It was quite the opposite. The Karen were accepted and everyone was very welcoming,' Mr Millington said.

A mentoring program was set up through the local neighbourhood house. 'People bent over backwards to help and we had 15 or 20 volunteers in no time. We were very fortunate that this community was prepared to help them,' he said.

Mr Millington's relationship with the Karen became such that he and his wife and daughters visited Thailand to attend the wedding of community leader Plaw Ganemy-Kunoo in the Mysot refugee camp on the Thai-Burma border.

They were smuggled into the camp at night and experienced first-hand the life of a displaced refugee. 'It was an incredible experience and it gives us credibility with the Karen and credibility to speak on their behalf,' Mr Millington said.

A WELCOMING COMMUNITY

One of the first Karen brought to settle in Nhill was Kaw Doh. He lived in a refugee camp on the Thai-Burma border for seven years and came to Australia as a refugee seven years ago. He and several other Karen moved from their community in Werribee to take up work in Nhill.

'I found it very different at first, I lived in a big house with ten to twenty people,' Kaw Doh said. 'Looking back it was a good experience, coming to live here (in Nhill). Melbourne was very expensive and here we had work. Since the Karen settled here eight families, including me, have bought houses. In Burma you can just build a house for yourself — every day is free, there is no rent and no insurance. You just build a house on communal land using bamboo and timber from the jungle. I miss my home, I miss the jungle and the rivers. But life here is good, I like living in Nhill and it's a good place for my family.'

THE ECONOMIC BENEFIT

Hindmarsh Shire Chief Executive Tony Doyle says Nhill has been enriched economically and culturally by the Karen. 'The social impact has been extraordinary but to see the way the community has embraced and open their hearts and minds has broadened everyone's thinking,' he said. 'We are all enriched because of the exposure to another culture and it has made Nhill a better place to live.'

He said the challenge for his and other rural shires is population decline, which can decimate local economies.

'In retail, shops close affecting the viability of the whole town. If you've got to go to Horsham to shop for something, you might as well do it all there,' Mr Doyle said. 'There is an impact on the ability of schools and hospitals to be funded and provide services. It affects business at all levels. The shire's funding is based on population levels and a decline has significant ramifications for us. The Karen community has provided an unskilled workforce which has allowed employment participation to grow enormously and feed back into services and shops in the community in a flow on effect. The Karen settlement has been really good for us. By allowing Luv-a-Duck to grow, it has increased the company's demand for more labour and essentially protected us from population decline.'

Mr Doyle said the council was preparing a community plan for the Karen and overall economic development strategy for the town. 'We could double the number of Karen if we had housing and jobs,' he said. Mr Doyle said the council planned to lead by example by ensuring it employed Karen.

'Nhill people are special and very community focused and they seem to embrace anyone who comes here. The Karen have had an extraordinary impact on transforming the lives of the people in the community they've joined. It's just an incredible story.'

An economic impact study by Deloitte Access Economics found that in its first two years the settlement program at Nhill had added 70 jobs and $40 million to the local economy.

'Win-win' is how the people of Nhill talk about the settlement of the Karen. The Karen have won jobs and a refuge; and the town has been given an economic and cultural transfusion.

Hal's employer Kim Moyle, owner of Halfway Motors, says the town has been given a new lease of life with the arrival of the Karen. 'We've noticed a big income difference since Hal began working here. The Karen bring their cars in because he works here and because we're the RACV agent and also because Hal can translate,' Ms Moyle said. 'Hal's a clever boy, he's keen to learn and now he's approaching his second year of an automotive Cert III qualification. He goes out on RACV call outs when rostered on and never complains. It is difficult to find skilled labour and Hal has been great for us. He's become part of the family and we take him everywhere. He loves Nhill and the space here and he loves his job. It was Hal's persistence that got him the job. He was a special kid.'

She said the settlement of the Karen had had a positive impact on Nhill. 'It's important for Nhill's future economically but Aussies can also learn a lot from them and their values of community and family. They're conscientious, kind and polite, they work hard and they're happy.'

CHAPTER 29
SINGING A SONG FOR FREEDOM

Quietly living and studying English in the south east Melbourne suburb of Dandenong is a man who, with his music, caused a wave of mass hysteria across a war-torn, fragmented nation.

In 2008 Navid Forogh won the Afghan Star talent competition — the equivalent of Australian Idol. At just 20 he became a youth culture sensation; Afghanistan's Justin Bieber. But with his success came a dreadful burden.

As the poster boy for a generation of Afghans who want a new, liberal, free and permissive way of life, Navid attracted the attention of the Taliban as well as conservative Muslim clerics. As he was driving home from a concert one night, he was fired at by a masked gunman; one bullet grazing his shoulder.

The majority of Afghans want a new, modern future but a violent minority — which includes the Taliban and other extremist Islamic groups — are trying to drag the country back to medieval culture and practice.

Conservative Islamic clerics also disapprove of popular music. Kabul's Mullah Abdullah told CNN earlier this year: 'There is no place for the music in Islam. We will not permit this westernised music in Afghanistan.'

But Navid said there was a groundswell among young Afghans who wanted to embrace Western culture.

'No matter what our enemies do, Afghans want to go forward. We want a future where anything is possible and we can be free to express ourselves through our art,' he said.

The Taliban banned all music for five years when they held power but now even women are singing popular music. One of Navid's rival finalists in the *Afghan Idol* competition was female pop singer Naweed Saberpoor.

Afghan Idol was first broadcast in 2002 but the 2009 season was the first to achieve wide popularity and criticism from conservative and extremist groups. It was produced under heightened security and watched by 11 million people — a third of the Afghan population. For many people, voting by phone for a favourite singer was their first taste of democracy.

Afghan Idol was created by entrepreneur Jahed Mohsini, who grew up in Australia. Presenter Doud Sediqi, who hosted the first three series, said the show's aim was to 'take people's hands from weapons to music'.

Navid also saw his Idol win as a means to unite and galvanise the youth of Afghanistan.

In his acceptance speech, he said: 'I want to thank all the people of Afghanistan for the votes. I was singing for everyone in this country no matter what their ethnic background. The young people of Afghanistan want to modernise and be more like the west while keeping our own cultural identity.'

After graduating from a mechanical high school in Kabul, Navid was running his family jewellery shop when he took up singing. He had released several albums in Afghanistan but his win on *Afghan Idol* catapulted him into serious national fame.

'I always loved singing and I seemed to have some talent for it but the Idol TV show really made my singing career grow,' Navid said.

His fame attracted the attention of the Taliban and he received death threats. 'I was told the Taliban wanted to kill me so my only option was to leave the country,' he said.

Navid fled to Dubai where he applied for and was granted a refugee visa by the Australian embassy, he has now settled into a house in Dandenong with some friends.

Navid is currently studying English and hoping to relaunch his music career. He has performed at concerts organised by the local Afghan community in Dandenong.

'I would like to meet some Australian musicians to learn about how the music industry works here and maybe get some advice,' Navid said. 'I love music and singing — it is my passion and would like very much to make a career in music.'

CHAPTER 30
NOOR'S STORY – PAYING A PRICE FOR EDUCATIONAL EQUALITY

In 2013 Pakistani schoolgirl Malala Yousafzai was awarded the European Parliament's *Sakharov Prize for Freedom of Though*t over her championing of girls' education.

As Malala's prize was being announced, Muhammad Noor was quietly living in a weatherboard cottage in Melbourne's west.

Muhammad, a teacher, also from Pakistan, fled his home country after being shot in the chest and left for dead by the Taliban after they took exception to his work educating girls.

Now he faces an uncertain future because of Australia's asylum seeker policies.

In 1996 Mr Noor founded a school for disadvantaged boys and girls.

'The Taliban told me I cannot teach girls, that this is against the Islamic way and that I should close my school,' Muhammad said. 'When I did not close, the Taliban came. They shot me and they destroyed my school with rocket propelled grenades.'

Neighbours rushed Muhammad to a local hospital, where he spent three months recovering. He is one of hundreds of thousands of Shia Muslims across the Middle East who have been subjected to persecution from governments or militant extremist groups.

After recovering from the assassination attempt and fleeing Pakistan, the 33-year-old worked in the United Arab Emirates as a construction supervisor until the government revoked the visas of more than 4,000 Shiite Muslims.

'When the government of the UAE cancelled the visas of all Shias and gave us one week to leave the country I was again forced to leave my home,' Muhammad said.

He paid $9,000 to a Malaysian people-smuggler to take him by boat to Australia, with the promise of a 'good, safe country'.

Muhammad said the boat trip was four nights and three days of constant fear.

'It was very difficult, there was no water or food and we got no chance to sleep. We all felt like the boat would sink and we would all die,' he said.

Muhammad's boat was rescued by the Royal Australian Navy and he was taken to Christmas Island. After a month in detention, he was released into the community in Adelaide and then made his way to Melbourne with a friend.

Mr Noor speaks five languages and recently has been working as a volunteer at his local church. Like around 30,000 other asylum seekers currently living in Australia he faces a wait to learn his fate. At the moment, the best he can hope for is a temporary protection visa, which means he has to reapply for protection every three years and may ultimately be forced to return home.

'If I go back to my country, the Taliban will be waiting for me. They will kill me because I challenged them over my school,' Muhammad said.

He now lives in a house in Melbourne's west, supported by AMES Australia and other community groups, sharing with four other asylum seekers.

He says he does not know what the future holds.

'We don't know what will happen. All we can do is pray.'

CHAPTER 31
FROM KILLING FIELDS TO MANSION GARDENS

James Brincat calls it his 'build it and they will come' moment. As the Ranger in Charge at Werribee Park, a former country estate in Melbourne's west, he has witnessed the regeneration of an historic garden and, in a remarkable example of cultural cross-pollination, the blossoming of local refugee communities. What started as a call for volunteers to help rebuild the gardens at Werribee turned into a therapy session for dislocated and isolated refugee families.

'It has been amazing to watch what has happened here,' James says, his passion and irrepressible nature evident in his voice. 'What started out as community project to rebuild the old kitchen garden here at Werribee Mansion has turned out to be an incredibly successful social experiment and a model for other community engagement projects. Everyone involved in this is blown away by what we've achieved and the inspirational outcomes that have come from putting some seeds in the ground and seeing what happens — both literally and figuratively.'

Like baseball fan Ray Kinsella in the Kevin Costner film *Field of Dreams*, James' garden was built to attract dislocated people from another time and place. And like the protagonist in the film, he built it and they came.

'We started with a working bee and we had a few of the local Karen people turn up to do some weeding in the mansion gardens. A few of them said they'd like to come back,' James said. 'The Karen came back with some their friends and family members and soon we had a small workforce.'

With so much labour on hand, James decided in June 2012 to recreate the Mansion's historic kitchen garden which was first established by the Chirnside family as owners of the mansion in 1875. The Chirnsides were one of Australia's wealthiest squatter families who created a pastoral empire in western Victoria and built the 60-room Italianate Werribee

Mansion between 1872 and 1877. As new laws and taxes were introduced into Australia and with the decline of the wool industry, the Chirnsides' fortunes waned and as a result the kitchen garden fell into disrepair. The family sold Werribee Park in 1922 and for many years the house served as a Catholic seminary.

In 1875 the garden produced fresh vegetables for the Chirnside's table; now it supplies Werribee Mansion's upscale restaurant with a stunning array of crops — from mustard greens to Vietnamese mint, capsicum and chard.

The garden is the result of a program called 'Working Beyond the Boundaries', a partnership between Parks Victoria, AMES and Werribee Mansion Hotel.

AMES program manager Dr Melika Yassin Sheikh-Eldin says that people from several emerging communities have been attracted to the park's volunteer program.

'Many of them have come from difficult circumstance or have spent years in refugee camps,' she said. 'Members of these communities, who are striving to adjust to a new country, are encouraged to join the program so that as well as garden they can learn new skills, develop social networks and gain an understanding of a new culture. The program has helped many people overcome health or social issues and it can offer a pathway to meaningful employment.'

The Karen people gravitated to the Werribee area after the first of them who arrived in Victoria as refugees were settled there. The ethnic minority Karen have been persecuted by the Burmese government for 30 years. There are an estimated 150,000 Karen living in refugee camps in or on the Thai border. The Burmese army have systematically destroyed Karen villages in operations described by human rights groups as ethnic cleansing.

A largely agrarian and village-based people, Karen refugees have often encountered difficulties when settled in urban locations around the world. Traditionally, they are gardeners and cultivators and living in an urban environment has left many of them dislocated and suffering depression. But being able to volunteer in the gardens of Werribee Park has had a remarkable effect on them.

James Brincat says that many of the local refugee communities have suffered clinical depression and that their health has improved because of the program.

'What we've seen is that people find a sense of self-worth being able to come here and do something constructive,' he said. 'What was a big surprise was to see the kids turn up — teenagers also — who want to come and garden. They're here during the school holidays and weekends, they just love being with their mums.'

One of the mums who played a key role in the success of the program is Evelyn Kunoo, who grew up in southern Burma with a large lush garden where her parents grew mangoes, bananas, pineapples and a cornucopia of vegetables. From the age of 17 and for 22 years Evelyn lived in a refugee camp on the Thai-Burma border. She and her husband Kert, whom she married in the camp, have been living in Hoppers Crossing for seven years.

James says Evelyn has been responsible for bringing people from the local refugee communities into the garden and inspiring them to contribute.

'Evelyn is a leader in her community and she has become the heart and soul of the garden. She has recruited and organised the community members to work in the gardens and is a driving force behind the whole thing,' he said.

Another key figure in the garden community, and one of its great success stories, is another Karen refugee Bee See Maw Kay. He spent many traumatic years in refugee camps in Thailand, lost his father and some of his family in the conflict there and has suffered depression and dislocation. Several months ago, 'Bee See' was without work and suffering severe depression. Now, thanks to the garden project at Werribee, BeeSee is an intern Park Ranger who hopes to become a fully-fledged Parks Victoria Ranger.

'At first Bee See was timid and almost afraid,' James said. 'But we've watched him blossom into a real leader in his community. He's gone from pulling up weeds to learning about machinery and he's studying horticulture.'

The program has seen the establishment of a private horticultural college at Werribee to provide training opportunities for members of local refugee communities to help them find paid work in the local market garden and nursery industries.

'Giving people from the communities skills they can translate into jobs is one the more rewarding aspects of being involved in the program,' he said.

James said the knowledge and skills exchange has been reciprocal. 'Our rangers say that having the Karen people work alongside them has been as much of a learning experience for them as for the volunteers.'

The local refugee communities in Wyndham, particularly the Karen, have taken to the job of managing the gardens in significant numbers and in doing so have found themselves re-engaged, with a new sense of purpose and reconnected with their traditional pursuits of gardening and food cultivation.

The project has become a model for both sustainable community gardens and engagement strategies for marginal communities; and, in the heart of one of Australia's rapidly developing urban districts, the Karen have rediscovered their links with the land.

Following the success of the kitchen garden, volunteers from local communities are now at work in park's orchard and river park. The orchard is home to hundreds of varieties of fruit and volunteers are involved in pruning, grafting and propagation work.

They are also working to help to stabilise river banks, reforest areas of woodland and humanely eradicate pests.

Field of Dreams is the story of an Iowa corn farmer who hears voices commanding him to build a baseball diamond in his fields. When he does, what appears is a ghostly team of long-lost baseball players none of whom ever reached their full potential. Anyone who has seen the film will know that the underlying theme is that for those prepared to open their hearts and minds, anything is possible. James Brincat and the volunteer gardeners of Werribee are proof of this. The gardens at Werribee have become a field of dreams for many people in local refugee communities. But unlike Ray Kinsella's *Field of Dreams*, James' garden is not a figment of imaginary Hollywood fancy, but a living, breathing, productive garden; and perhaps more importantly the cultural and spiritual focus for a group of people lost in time and space.

CHAPTER 32
BATOOR'S JOURNEY — AWARD WINNING PHOTOS HIGHLIGHT A PEOPLE'S PLIGHT

When Afghan Hazara refugee Barat Ali Batoor won the inaugural 'Photo of the Year' in the prestigious Nikon-Walkley Press Photography awards, it was the vindication of a career spent giving a voice to the vulnerable.

Barat Ali Batoor's photo 'The First Day at Sea' was entered as part of a photo essay on asylum seekers travelling the people-smuggling route from Indonesia. It was published in the *Global Mail*.

Batoor accompanied a group of asylum seekers on a hazardous and ill-fated boat journey from a remote Indonesian island to Christmas Island in September 2012. On the trip the boat started to sink and Batoor and others swam to a nearby island where they were arrested by Indonesian police.

'I was very excited to have won this award,' Batoor said. 'I'm pleased to have been able to show the real story behind these journeys — to show how people are risking their lives and enduring perils to escape persecution and the threat of death in the home countries. I just tried my best to show what is really happening. My hope was that my pictures would tell that story. This award is not about me, but a confirmation that I could tell the stories of my people to the world. These journeys mix fear, boredom and extreme loneliness. They sometimes end happily, sometimes in despair and sometimes in death. I was lucky. I survived and I was quickly found to be a refugee and resettled in Australia.'

Before coming to Australia he worked as a photojournalist in Afghanistan. He produced a series of pictures, published in the *Washington Post*, about 'The Dancing Boys of Afghanistan' who were essentially young men kidnapped into sexual slavery by Afghan warlords and tribal leaders. Because of these photos and his work with the western press, he was forced to flee Afghanistan.

Batoor's family had fled Afghanistan forty years earlier because of persecution and set up home to Quetta, Pakistan, a city that hosts a large population of displaced Hazara.

He returned to Afghanistan in 2001 at just 18 years of age after he was hired by a photographer and a journalist working for the British newspaper *The Sunday Telegraph* to be their interpreter. It was the beginning of a journey that would change Batoor's life.

'When I went to Afghanistan and saw the destruction and devastation, I wanted to do something. Then I saw the foreign photojournalists working and realised that if I could also become a photographer, I might be able to help the country. I used the money I made as an interpreter to buy my first camera,' Batoor said.

He returned again to Afghanistan in 2005 this time on his own terms as a photojournalist.

But the publication of the 'Dancing Boys' story also brought the death threats and in 2012 Batoor moved his family back to Quetta.

The situation in Pakistan was not much better, though. Other ethnic groups were boycotting Hazaras; they were being denied access to education, work and even the ability to walk to the local bazaar. Batoor realised the only way he could support his mother, brothers and sisters was to find work in another country. He met with a people smuggler, paid his money and began a journey to Australia.

Himself part of the exodus, Batoor began documenting the displacement of his own Hazara people as they fled from Afghanistan and Pakistan to safety abroad.

The Hazara are a Persian-speaking mostly Shia Muslim minority that is the third-largest ethnic group in Afghanistan. They have been persecuted in Afghanisatan for centuries.

So, in September 2012, Batoor became part of the story, fleeing with his camera in hand. Travelling with 92 other passengers hidden below deck to escape detection by Indonesian water police, he shot a selection of images capturing the long route through Thailand, Malaysia,

Indonesia and by sea to Australia.

'It is a journey of sudden midnight departures, long road trips, surreptitious transactions, treks through jungles, and terror at sea,' Batoor said, of his photo essay. 'Few people — except for the refugees themselves — ever get to see this reality.'

The first night of the journey was calm, but by the second night the conditions at sea began to deteriorate.

'The water was very rough, and then the bilge pump stopped working. Those who were not seasick tried to remove the water in buckets, but more water was coming in than going out,' Batoor said. 'Our boat was floating like a matchbox. There was screaming, shouting and crying. Everybody lost hope and we were thinking that this was the end and that everyone was dying.'

Batoor's boat ran aground on the rocks and his camera was ruined but remarkably, his images survived. He was then detained and robbed by Indonesian authorities but escaped. Many of the other people he met on his arduous journey didn't survive.

'I am very lucky,' he said. 'Unlike most Hazaras, I was quickly found to be a refugee. I just kept taking photos; my hope is that, at the very least, these pictures can tell their story.'

Shortly before getting on the boat to Christmas Island, Batoor had met with Aubrey Belford, a Jakarta-based journalist from *The Global Mail* news website. Belford gave him his card and suggested they stay in touch.

On his return to Indonesia and with little money, no shoes and on the run, Batoor contacted Belford and they met at dawn on a Jakarta street. Belford realised the potential of Batoor's story and, more particularly, his photos and they were published that week in *The Global Mail*.

Soon after, SBS aired a half-hour documentary on Batoor and other Hazara asylum seekers for *Dateline*, giving the Australian public a close look at the circumstances of asylum seekers seeking safety.

Batoor's application through the UNHCR for refugee status was expedited because of his journalist friends and media coverage he received. He arrived in Australia in 2013.

He is currently planning to release a film on his experiences.

CHAPTER 33
A NEW LEASE ON LIFE FOR REFUGEE FAMILY

For Syrian refugees Tawfik and Ghunwa Mira settling in Melbourne has not just given them safety and a chance to rebuild their lives, it has also given them back their son.

The couple's 11-year-old boy Yousef suffers from cerebral palsy and epilepsy. For the first ten years of his life, Yousef was mostly asleep and largely unresponsive when he wasn't. Doctors in Syria advised the family to give Yousef sleeping pills.

For the past four years the family has struggled to get medicines and treatment for Yousef; firstly because of the conflict in their home country and secondly because their status as refugees in Lebanon afforded them no access to free medical care.

'Yousef was asleep most of the time, he was lying down and not responsive at all. It was like I had a child but I didn't have a child,' Ghunwa said.

Upon their arrival in Australia, Yousef spent a month as a patient at the Royal Children's Hospital where his condition was stabilised and a treatment and therapy plan was formulated. After three-and-a-half months in Australia, his quality of life has improved significantly.

'The change is massive. Now Yousef can move his head and hands. He can hear voices and noises,' Ghunwa said. 'It's very nice to see Yousef now, I never dreamed of seeing him strong and happy and more alert. His epilepsy episodes are much less. The staff at the Royal Children's Hospital and the people from the refugee agency AMES have been fantastic. When we arrived Yousef was like a dead body, he could do nothing. Now, it's as if he has entered our lives for the first time. It's like we've got our son back. I feel like a mother for the first time and it is amazing that Yousef is attending Glenroy Special School five a days a week.'

The Mira family have shared their epic journey from the war-torn streets of Aleppo to life in limbo as refugees in Lebanon and finally to a safe new home in Melbourne's northern suburbs. The family has survived one of the most brutal and bloody conflicts of recent times, they have endured life on the margins as refugees in a country that didn't want them and they have overcome the tragedy of the death of their youngest son.

'Before the war, Aleppo was a beautiful ancient city and also one of the biggest cities for industry in the Arab world,' Tawfik said. 'When the conflict between the Syrian army and the rebel armies started and the fighting came to our neighbourhood, we had to leave.'

The Mira family moved from one place to another to seek safety but every time they moved the fighting followed, forcing Tawfik to give up his work as a stonemason.

'We had little food and no medicine for the children,' Tawfik said.

The Mira family lived for two years in an underground shelter as bombs rained down on the city outside.

'Because I had two disabled kids meant I didn't go outside. Tawfik went out when we needed food,' Ghunwa said.

Then one day the family was told there was a way out; a dangerous two-day bus journey that would deliver them to safety in Lebanon.

'We took the bus. It was a dangerous trip but it was a way to escape the war. We had to carry the children,' Tawfik said.

But life in Lebanon was only marginally better for the family and they struggled to make ends meet living frugally in the small village of Mashtura.

'The way they treated us as refugees in Lebanon was very bad. They had the attitude that we were bad people,' Ghunwa said.

It was in Lebanon that they tragically lost their other son, three-and-a-half year-old Ali who suffered from a condition similar to Yousef's.

'Ali got sick and passed away. He had a chest infection but the doctors in Lebanon would not treat him because he was disabled,' Ghunwa said. 'They told me to take him home and let him die… and they wouldn't let me bury him. They said you are not from Lebanon, you do not have a place here to bury him.'

The family registered as refugees with the United Nations in Lebanon and were eventually offered a resettlement place in Australia. But they almost didn't make it. Just before they left, Yousef became ill and was taken to hospital. He spent 15 days in in the clinic and the Lebanese health authorities refused to release him unless the family paid $US1,500 for medical expenses. Eventually the Australian Embassy paid the bill and the family were able to travel to Australia.

The Miras say they are happy and grateful to be in Australia and are keen to find work and contribute to the society that has given them a safe haven. But their family and friends are scattered because of the war.

'We have no idea where many of them are,' Tawfik said. 'I have one brother in Turkey and another still in Lebanon and my mother is still in Syria. I worry about her.'

CHAPTER 34
REFUGEE'S ART PROVIDES ECONOMIC AND EMOTIONAL SUSTENANCE

Sketching portraits of shoppers and festival goers earned Syrian refugee Nouha Saigh just enough money to feed her family and pay the rent. Nearly destitute in Lebanon having fled her home and prosperous life in war-ravaged Aleppo, Nouha relied on her talents as an artist to support herself and her five children.

'I would go out to the shops or to festival and I would sketch people's portraits for a small amount of money. At that time, it was all we had but it was enough to pay the rent and feed my children,' Nouha said.

Fifty-year-old Syrian refugee Nouha has been painting and drawing since she was four and she says art was an emotional as well as economic support for her in desperate times. She studied art in her home town of Aleppo and found inspiration for her work in the ancient and beautiful streets of the historic city and among its cosmopolitan population.

But in 2012 Nouha was forced to flee her beloved city when war came. Aleppo was a centre of resistance to the brutal Assad regime and a deadly civil war erupted as government forces attacked the rebels. As a result of the battles, many parts of the Old City of Aleppo World Heritage Site, including parts of the Great Mosque of Aleppo and other medieval buildings in the ancient city, were destroyed and ruined. Nouha says Aleppo became a dangerous place where life was cheap and the beauty of the city's architecture and history held no value for the combatants.

'Before the war we had a very active and happy life in Syria. I worked in a commercial bank and as an artist. I was very happy. I went to work every day, cooked dinner for my family and spent hours drawing,' Nouha said. 'Our life was good before the war. We had many friends and we would go on picnics, go dancing and go to restaurants. But when the war came that all stopped. It became very dangerous.'

Nouha and her family saw the conflict close up when a bomb exploded in their kitchen and another in their backyard.

'Many people were killed. It was a terrible time and very frightening,' she said.

The family fled and attempted to go to Turkey.

'When we were crossing the border into Turkey we were stopped by some militia who threatened to kill us. I thought we were all going to die,' she said.

Nouha, a devout Christian, prayed and when the driver of one of the militia's trucks intervened the family was allowed to cross into Turkey.

'We didn't know where we were going to go or where we would sleep,' she said.

They were given shelter in a church but could not get official recognition from Turkish authorities and eventually decided to go to Lebanon. The family arrived there with just $US50.

'We had no money and so I would go to the shopping areas or to festivals and sketch people's portraits for a little bit of money,' Nouha said. 'It was just enough to pay for the rent and buy some food.'

In July 2014 Nouha and her family were accepted for resettlement in Australia.

She says that art is her passion and is now both an important link back to her heritage in Syria and a way of celebrating the 'sunshine' coming to live in Australia has provided her family.

'I love Australia because Australia has helped my family and I love Australia because of the beautiful sunshine and colourful landscapes you have here,' Nouha said. 'Also the people here are very kind and helpful.'

Some of Nouha's art was accepted into the *Heartlands 2017 Art Project*, an exhibition of works by refugee artists. Her work reflects the dire situation in Syria and the suffering being endured by its people. Nouha hopes to continue her career as an artist in Melbourne.

'My aim is to tell the world, through my art, about the suffering of the Syrian people and their hopes for peace,' she said.

CHAPTER 35
BLOOD FEUDS, BATTLES AND BANDITS — A REFUGEE'S JOURNEY

Unlike the armed-to-the-teeth Australian soldiers alongside him, young Afghan Nabi went into combat wielding only his language skills.

Nabi worked for three years as an interpreter for Australian, Dutch and US forces in Oruzgan Province, Afghanistan, as they attempted to neutralise Taliban fighting units while training up local soldiers in the Afghan National Army (ANA). As a speaker of the four major language groups in Afghanistan and also fluent in English, he was a key man for Australian troops there in being able to communicate with their Afghan counterparts as well as civilian officials.

His is a life marked by Dickensian drudgery, Shakespearean tragedy, and a medieval-style blood feud. In his 32 years, Nabi has had to flee his home four times; he's been targeted by extremist groups, forced as a 12-year-old to sell fruit on the streets to feed his family and he's survived two wars. But he's also rubbed shoulders with Prime Ministers and NATO commanders and held down key jobs with western military and diplomatic organisations. His father was murdered as a result of a 35-year-old tribal quarrel. But he is now living in Melbourne as a refugee and has four children of his own.

Nabi's story is one full of incredible resilience, unbridled optimism and good humour; and as many twists and turns as the mountain paths of his homeland.

'My father was a Tajik from the Panjshir Valley, in the north of Afghanistan, but I grew up in Kabul,' Nabi said. 'He was a Mujahideen who fought against the Russians but he had to flee the country eventually to escape them. He went to Pakistan — to a place called Khyber Pakhtunkhwa (KPK) Province on the border with

Afghanistan — and once known as North-West Frontier Province. My mother and siblings and I joined him there and that's where I started school and began learning languages and where I came across English for the first time.'

But when the Russians left and the communist regime collapsed the family moved back to Kabul in 1991. Nabi was six.

'At that time in Pakistan, my father was a senior Mujahideen and we often hosted fighters in our house as they passed through on their way to fight the Russians,' Nabi said.

Back in his home city Nabi resumed his schooling until the arrival of the Taliban in the late 1990s.

'There were problems; my father was a Tajik and my mother was Pashtun which is an unusual thing in Afghanistan. When they married it wasn't a problem but it became a subject of tension,' Nabi said. 'And then one day there were some Pakistani Taliban fighters playing cricket on our school ground. I went to tell them that we needed the ground to play football and one of them slapped me and abused me. My mother stopped me from going to that school.'

During the Taliban's reign Nabi's father became a target because of his Tajik ethnicity and was forced to flee the country again.

'He was detained by the Taliban for a month and was beaten so badly he couldn't walk. When they let him go, he fled to Pakistan,' he said.

This left Nabi as head of the family and, at the age of 12, responsible for the livelihoods of his five sisters, brother, mother and step-mother.

'I became the man of the family as the eldest son and I had to do everything because the Taliban would not let females out of the houses where they lived,' he said.

Nabi's father had a shop selling shoes and other goods but it failed under the strict regulations of the Taliban and when the family had exhausted its savings, Nabi was forced to sell fruit and cigarettes on the street to makes ends meet.

'This was a tough time in my life, my education had been basically stopped, my family had lost everything and when our money ran out I was forced to work selling on the streets,' he said. 'The Taliban were always questioning me about my father but I had no idea where he had gone. But I always wanted to study and I dreamed that I would have a bright future and that I could maybe get somewhere and be a success.'

When a message came from his father that he was alive and well in Pakistan, Nabi travelled there alone as a 13-year-old at the urging of his 90-year-old grandfather, who wanted news of his own son.

'So, I went to Pakistan. It was a new experience for me; I had never travelled so far alone before. I found my father but he could not come back to Afghanistan because of the Taliban and when I got back to Kabul my grandfather had died. He died not having seen his son (my father) again.'

Forced by their penurious circumstances to sell the family house and with little money and fewer prospects, Nabi took his family to Pakistan to be with his father.

They lived for two years in a refugee camp at Nasir Bagh, which became famous when the photograph of Afghan girl Sharbat Gula with her piercing green eyes appeared on the cover of *National Geographic* magazine in June 1985. The camp was closed in 2002.

Nabi tried to study a little in the camp but he and his father worked as labourers to support the family.

His father was forced to flee yet again when some Pakistan-based extremists learned of his presence in the area. This time they fled to Iran.

'The local Taliban intelligence people in Pakistan were looking for my father so he went to Quetta and then to Iran. We had no word from him for a year and a half,' Nabi said.

At 14 or 15 he was again the head of the family and working hard to take care of everyone. Finally, a message and some money came from Iran.

'My father sent money and asked me to bring the family to Iran. I gave half of it to a smuggler and we went to Iran in 1999,' Nabi said. 'We found my father and we lived there in reasonably good conditions until 2004. My father and I worked as painters and labouring in construction and we could live quite well compared to the camp.'

It was in Iran that Nabi fell in love with the English language.

'I had friend in Iran also from Afghanistan who had been an English teacher in Kabul and I asked him to help me improve my English. He gave me some books and we talked in English and I fell in love with the language,' Nabi said.

With the ejection of the Taliban from Kabul and the establishment of the Karzai regime in 2004, Nabi's family returned home.

'We had a little money we had saved in Iran so we could resettle in Afghanistan. We rented a house and looked for jobs,' Nabi said. 'It was really tough to find a job and I ended up labouring again and selling fruit.'

Nabi said his father had the opportunity to work for the Karzai Government but declined because of his stance against corruption.

Back in Kabul, Nabi resumed his studies as he worked to support his family. But then almost for the first time in his short life of fear, drudgery and exile, opportunity came knocking. Through the recommendation of a cousin who was working with the ANA, Nabi was offered a job as an interpreter with Dutch coalition forces.

'I took a bus to Kandahar and took a chopper flight to the air base in Oruzgan with the Dutch officer who hired me. Sitting in front of me was a US four star general,' Nabi said.

He ended up working with Australian, Dutch, US and French army units translating their conversations with Afghan troops and local officials.

'I went to the battlefield with these people. I was in body armour on the front line alongside them,' Nabi said.

He worked with Australia's special operations Task Force 66 which was tasked with eliminating key Taliban leaders and also with Australian soldiers posted to the Reconstruction Task Force (RTF) who were building schools, hospitals and repairing infrastructure.

Nabi tells of being on one operation to capture a Taliban explosives engineer.

'It was four in the morning and commandos had surrounded a compound looking for this man. There was fire fight and two Afghan soldiers were killed,' he said. 'It was very scary and confusing but I survived it.'

He spent three and half years in the field working long hours alongside coalition troops and became invaluable because he was able to speak Pashtu, Dari and English. But as Nabi's fortunes improved, tragedy struck. His father was murdered by a cousin; the result of a 35-year-old tribal blood feud.

'After I got this job my father was shot dead by one of his cousins. It was something to do with a quarrel and some tribal tensions that started 35 years earlier,' Nabi said. 'My father was not really involved but because he was related to one of the people who was involved, he was targeted. It was terrible. I was very close to my father and I was again the only person to hold the family together. At that time I challenged myself to do everything I could to help my family.'

In 2009 Nabi was offered an office job as supervisor of the US army's interpreters in Oruzgan Province and subsequently met some Australia diplomats who offered him a job with the Department of Foreign Affairs and Trade (DFAT). He joined DFAT as a language and cultural advisor in 2011, helping to deliver Australia's aid and reconstruction program in Afghanistan.

'I loved this job. I was able to provide advice about local cultural and political matters and I could also understand the Aussie accent because I had worked with Australian soldiers,' Nabi said. 'These DFAT people were different from the military. They were very professional and very committed. I was proud of the work we did.

'I attended meetings with provincial officials and senior coalition officers talking about issues around development, health care and education. I really enjoyed the work and met some great people. I was very happy,' he said.

In his new role, he met Prime Ministers Malcolm Turnbull and Julia Gillard and Defence Minister Stephen Smith; and even the commander of US forces in Afghanistan Stanley McChrystal.

Recently married and with a new family, Nabi got a job at the Australian embassy in Kabul liaising with Afghan government officials. But his return to his home city was not without its problems.

'The people who had killed my father had joined the Taliban to escape justice and then they came after me,' Nabi said. 'They put a tag on me and my family as a supporter of the 'infidels', the 'invaders' because I had worked for the coalition. Life became very dangerous for me and my family.'

So when the Australian Government offered resettlement visas to people who had worked with Australian forces in Afghanistan, Nabi had no option but to apply for one. He put in a request to have his extended family — including his mother and sisters — to come to Australia. But it was refused and only his own immediate family were issued visas.

His wife and three children arrived in Melbourne in August 2016 and since then they have had another daughter. Nabi has undertaken a course for professional migrants and is now looking for work and planning further study.

'I am very happy to be here. My family is safe and my kids have a chance to do whatever they want,' he said. 'I also have a chance to be successful. I would love to work helping other migrants and to give back to Australia. That is my dream.'

Karen refugees have settled in the small town of Nhill, in western Victoria, finding jobs and futures for themselves and breathing much needed life into the struggling regional town (chapter 28).

The gardens at Werribee Park, in Melbourne's west, have become a haven for local refugee communities whose volunteering efforts have restored the historic patch of greenery (chapter 31).

Afghan photographer Barat Ali Batoor's work in depicting his own refugee journey saw him win Australia's premier award for photojournalism (chapter 32).

As one of Africa's 'lost boys', Peter Kon was taken from his family's South Sudanese village as a small boy. After surviving hunger, war and two decades in refugee camps, he has carved out a new life for himself in Australia (chapter 48).

As displaced refugees Syrian couple Tawfik and Ghunwa Mira struggled to get medicines and treatment for their profoundly disabled son Yousef. Now in Melbourne and with proper treatment and therapy they say they have been given back their boy (chapter 33).

Displaced by war from her affluent life in the historic city of Aleppo, sketching portraits of shoppers and festival goers earned Syrian refugee artist Nouha Saigh just enough money to feed her family and pay the rent (chapter 34).

As an interpreter for Australian forces in Afghanistan Nabi saw the conflict close up. But ironically when the fighting ended, his work with coalition troops meant he had to flee after being targeted by Taliban sympathisers (chapter 35).

Hal Loo at Nhill. Photo courtesy of Hindmarsh Shire Council (chapter 28).

After fleeing civil war in the late 1970s, Eritrean refugee Melika Yassin Sheikh-Eldin has completed a doctorate, set up refugee-centred social enterprises and helped thousands of new arrivals to Australia settle successfully (chapter 25).

After more than a decade in a refugee camp and battles with depression and learning disabilities, Karen-Burmese refugee Eh Hta Dah Shee has finally found his place in the world (chapter 36).

Clare Pritchard runs a small group of mostly mums from Melbourne's Dandenong Ranges that supports vulnerable refugees and asylum seekers (chapter 38).

As a doctor working in Iraq during the conflict there, Asseel Yako saved hundreds of lives. His work was tending to battlefield wounds suffered by soldiers or militia members fighting ISIS; or patching up women and children horrifically injured in explosions or gunfire. After escaping the maelstrom of war, he is now resuming his career in Australia (chapter 43).

Afghan refugee Mirwais Janbaz's first brush with death came at just seven years of age. He was just ten metres from the shop his mother had sent him to buy bread from when a bomb exploded killing everyone inside (chapter 44).

Somali student and photographer Abdullahi Ibrahim has used the camera lens to capture the essence of refugee communities (chapter 27).

Najaf Mazari says that there are very few Afghans who can remember a time when there was not fighting. The Afghan refugee and author of the best-selling memoir *The Rugmaker of Mazar-e-Sharif* came to Australia in an asylum seeker boat in 2001 and has rebuilt his life in Melbourne (chapter 41).

South Sudanese singer Ajak Kwai shares, through her music, her own story and the rich culture of her people. As a proud Dinka woman, singing and storytelling are central to maintaining her connection to her people and their cultural traditions (chapter 42).

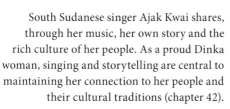

Vedran Drakulic spent most of the Bosnian war helping others. When the time came and he was the one needing help, he gratefully accepted Australia's offer of a safe haven. Since then, he has been giving back to the country that gave him a chance to start a new life (chapter 47).

Vietnamese refugee Hao Quach steered a rickety boat across stormy seas filled with pirates on an epic journey to safety and salvation (chapter 46).

Kosovar-Albanian refugee Mirisha Bowler has found peace and acceptance in Australia after a remarkable journey through war, the loss of loved ones and exile from her homeland (chapter 49).

CHAPTER 36
COURAGE AND RESILIENCE REVEALED IN A SMILE

They say a smile is the light in the window of your soul. For Karen refugee Eh Hta Dah Shee, his beaming face belies a lifetime of struggle, deprivation and hardship. After more than a decade in a refugee camp and battles with depression and learning disabilities, his infectious grin says that the he's finally found his place in the world.

The 25-year-old, known affectionately as 'Dutchie', has spent the past four years volunteering at Werribee Park Mansion and at Serendip wildlife sanctuary, in Melbourne's west.

Dutchie's new found lease on life is largely because of a volunteering program run by Parks Victoria and migrant and refugee settlement agency AMES Australia called 'Working Beyond the Boundaries', which is designed to help members of the local refugee communities gain the skills and confidence necessary to find employment.

Werribee Park head ranger James Brincat says Dutchie is fluent in English, Karen and speaks Thai yet he cannot read and write.

'He has learnt all of these languages through a kind of osmosis,' Mr Brincat said. 'Dutchie has a learning disability and has special needs yet he has been able to achieve an incredible amount in terms of being able to learn how the gardens here operate and he is making an amazing contribution.'

After leaving school Dutchie suffered isolation and depression. 'As all of his siblings have now left home, so he was spending all of his day-time at home alone, bored and lonely,' Mr Brincat said. 'His mother encouraged him to volunteer here at the gardens as there are many Karen here and his mother thought would be good for him to make a contribution to the community and perhaps being with the park rangers may help boost his confidence. Since he started with us his English is now fluent and he is more confident in communicating with Europeans.'

Dutchie says working at Werribee Park has given him purpose and a meaningful life.

'I am very happy here. It is good to come here and do something. I love working with plants and working with the people here is good,' he said.

He said life in the refugee camp was very tough; and his first years in Australia were only slightly easier with making friends proving difficult.

He arrived in Australia aged 13, the youngest of five siblings. Like many Karen who found their way to Australia, his family had lived in Mae La refugee camp in Thailand's Tak province, near the Burma border. Dutchie said the area around the camp was a violent place.

'The people were fighting or hurting each other, and when I came here I was scared of people… They kill each other, they don't care. No one cares about it. They pull them to the side of the road and just leave them,' he said. 'There was not much to do and no opportunities but life is much better here for us. In Thailand I knew nothing about growing plants and I could not speak English but now I am learning about horticulture and I can speak to people in Australia in English. Also I was very shy and nervous when I came to Australia but now I am more confident and happy.'

But he said at first, he was uncertain about volunteering in the garden. 'When I first started I was shy and nervous when I saw the people, the new people. I used to look down at the ground when the people talked to me — I was shy and tried hide. Now I am getting good. I can speak with the people. When I was in Thailand I did not imagine that Australia would be like this, that I would be here in the country growing vegetables. I am very lucky,' he said.

Hundreds of thousands of Karen people were killed in the conflict and about 140,000 made it across the border to refugee camps in Thailand. Just over 3,000 have been settled in Victoria.

Many Karen refugees volunteer in at Werribee Park growing vegetables, pruning and weeding as well as looking after the chooks. Each month 3,500 volunteer hours are essential to the upkeep of Werribee Park's extensive grounds and facilities.

CHAPTER 37
ESCAPING THE HORRORS OF THE SYRIAN CONFLICT

A woman who witnessed first-hand the horrors of the Syrian conflict and was forced to flee her home in the war-torn nation has been reunited with her sons in Melbourne.

Amina Srio, a Syrian refugee who fled her home in the besieged town of Aleppo and took refuge in neighbouring Lebanon for several months, was met by her two sons and their families at Melbourne Airport on 9 March in the climax to a remarkable human story.

As she was travelling inside Syria to avoid the fighting, she became caught up in it.

'I was travelling between one city and another when armed men attacked the bus I was on,' Amina said. 'I was not hurt but I saw the lady beside me without her head and covered in blood. It was terrible and I was in hysteria.'

Amina's son Rasheed Rustom, who has been in Melbourne for eight years, has been trying to bring his mother to Australia since the conflict in Syria broke out.

'We had tried to get her here — even just on a visitor visa — but with no success,' Rasheed said. 'At first we had to get her out of her house and move her to safer places within Syria and then we had to get her out of Syria altogether,' he said.

Amina travelled to Lebanon where she rented a room in a hotel. 'I was on my own and I didn't know anyone... and I didn't feel that safe in Lebanon,' she said.

Rasheed considered getting his mother to Indonesia and then meeting her there and bringing her to Australia on an asylum seeker boat. 'In the beginning I was scared of the idea but after the attack on the bus, I agreed,' Amina said.

Ultimately Amina was able to come to Australia through the Community Proposal Pilot program under the sponsorship of settlement agency AMES. The scheme cost Rasheed and his brother $20,000 in fees and a $5,000 refundable bond but they consider it money well spent.

'For the first week I couldn't believe she was really here and I'm still pinching myself,' Rasheed said. 'We are thankful for getting our mother to safety, we will be grateful forever.'

The Community Proposal Pilot (CPP) is an unfunded humanitarian entrant program of 1,000 places which began in July 2013.

AMES, as an Approved Proposing Organisation (APO), works with Australian community members who have friends or family members who have fled their home country due to significant discrimination and/or persecution and proposes their visa applications to the Department of Immigration and Border Protection.

Rasheed said he didn't tell his mother about the cost of the program because she would not have agreed to come. But Amina is delighted to be in Melbourne with her sons. 'I'm really happy now, being here is beyond description — it's a great place to live,' she said.

CHAPTER 38
SMALL ACTS OF KINDNESS MAKING A BIG DIFFERENCE

The majestic Mountain Ash forests of the Dandenong Ranges are a long way from the mangrove swamps of Manus Island and the coral outcrops of Nauru. But scattered among the tree ferns and messmate stands around the townships of Monbulk and Kallista live the members of a small volunteer group that has had a big impact on the lives of people who have suffered as a result of being caught up in Australia's system of offshore immigration detention.

'*Kindred*' is a group of like-minded people, mostly mums, from the local area who are concerned about Australia's asylum seeker policies and want not only to help those affected but also to see them changed. The group has vision for a kinder and more compassionate society in which communities are the driving force of a spirit that would see asylum seekers welcomed in Australia.

Clare Pritchard was one of the founders of the group and her work with Kindred saw her nominated for an award at the 2017 Australian Settlement and Migration Awards. She has a background in social work and has worked in trauma counselling. She now teaches yoga locally in the Dandenongs and also specialises in trauma sensitive yoga, which provides an opportunity for victims to safely experiment with breathing, moving, strengthening, stretching and resting; regaining control of their own bodies. She works part time at the Western Region Centre Against Sexual Assault in Footscray and at CASA House at the Royal Women's Hospital. Clare is also a member of the detention advocacy team at the Asylum Seeker Resource Centre. But her passion over the past few years has been Kindred.

Clare said the death of Iranian asylum seeker Reza Barati, who was murdered in Papua New Guinea in 2014, was the spark that created the group.

'When this young man was killed we just felt compelled to do something. So we put out an invitation for people to come and meet at the yoga room and we lit a candle in his honour,' she said. 'A handful of women came who were concerned about the issue. We didn't really know what we could do but we realised we needed to do something.'

The women of Kindred eventually settled on four avenues of action: advocacy, material aid, fundraising and direct support. The fourth avenue has largely meant having volunteers visit detainees at Melbourne Immigration Transit Accommodation (MITA) in Broadmeadows to provide friendship and support in a casual informal way. But Clare says it has sometimes been difficult for volunteers in the group to see 'the cold hard face of the detention system'.

'These are not trained case managers and the experiences some volunteers have visiting people who are the victims of trauma can be mind-blowing,' she said. 'It's difficult because we go in and visit and then we leave and the detainees are left. That's a cause of self-reflection for a lot of people. And of course, it's not normal friendship — you can't really have a normal friendship with someone locked in detention or even someone on a bridging visa whose future is uncertain. I think it is a case of constantly checking in with our own position of privilege and power and consciously trying to mitigate that in every interaction. It is about recognising the dire situation that our friends are in, something that we can just never fully understand, and finding a way to connect based on our shared humanity.'

Clare said working as a small volunteer organisation in a very intense and difficult area meant energy levels sometimes waxed and waned.

'At one point we were trying to do anything and everything and after a while that becomes wearing and is not sustainable,' she said. 'It can have a big impact on those dealing with vulnerable people and some of the people we've supported are very traumatised. So, we've been mindful that the people doing this work need to be looked after and that it's OK to step back for a bit and say that "this is getting to me".'

But the efforts of Kindred volunteers have had a positive impact and the group also now has a focus on community engagement, through material aid collections and fundraising events. The group's Facebook page now has hundreds of followers in the Dandenong Ranges and across Melbourne.

'Part of our commitment is to raise awareness but we also try to help in a practical way. The beauty of a small group is that if someone needs $200 we can respond to that sort of thing quickly. Mostly, our call outs for support get overwhelming responses,' Clare said.

She said the power of 'real stories and real family' has helped the group build public awareness of issues around asylum policies.

Clare tells the story of one Nauru detainee who became distraught when his father-in-law threatened to remarry his wife unless he was able to send money to support the family.

'The man obviously had no access to money to send home so we posted a Facebook call out and we were able to raise some money to sort things out,' she said.

Clare says the strength of Kindred's volunteering model was its flexibility.

'We don't ask people to commit for a certain number of hours, they can contribute what they're comfortable with. And all of the money donated doesn't go into a big pool; it goes directly to the people needing it,' she said.

Clare says as Kindred has grown, she and her colleagues have been humbled and grateful for the generosity, energy and compassion being shown by supporters.

'Kindred has really been a lot about bringing people together,' she said. 'And for me and my family; we've been enriched by so many of the people we've met.'

CHAPTER 39
OVERCOMING ABUSE — A WOMAN'S JOURNEY TO SELF-RELIANCE

Ritu Dhar is a refugee — not from armed conflict but from an abusive arranged marriage.

As an escapee from an abusive arranged marriage alone in a strange country with no money, no job and a 15-month-old child, life looked grim for the Indian migrant. Subjected to emotional and financial abuse and prohibited from doing almost anything without her overbearing husband's permission, she faced an invidious choice; buckle down obediently or go home to India in disgrace.

But the 42-year-old's inspirational journey from near destitution to successful, independent woman stands as an example for other women who are the victims of abusive relationships; and as a testament to her own resilience.

She spent a year carefully planning her escape from abuse and servitude and has spent the next decade building a future for herself and her son. She slowly put together the documents she would need and even collected spare change so she would have her own money when the time came for her to leave. 'I was determined my son and I would have a life of our own and I started working towards that. I knew I had the will power to make it happen,' Ritu said.

Originally from Kashmir, Ritu grew up in a middle-class family in New Delhi. After graduating with an arts degree and studying an MBA she worked in a series of office jobs. Then in 2002, in an arranged marriage, she wed an Indian professional living in Australia.

'I was married at age 30, which is quite late for Indian women,' Ritu said. 'I was very scared even to travel by aeroplane alone. I had been very protected and insulated in India which is a very conservative society. There was no nightlife, no boyfriends. I had always dreamed of living in a foreign land but because I wasn't an engineer or a doctor people thought I wasn't worth anything. In India as a woman you are not allowed to do what you want. I was well educated but the only jobs I could get were admin or reception roles. I wanted something better in life but that better thing never came. So, I was very happy to get married but I knew nothing of Australia or its people. I was scared that people wouldn't be able to understand me even though I had a good command of English. And I really didn't know how to talk to Australians or how the society worked.'

As soon as Ritu arrived in Australia, things went sour and she realised her husband was not the man she thought she had married.

'My husband was overbearing and controlling. He just didn't want to know about my dreams and ambitions. And my life was so controlled that I might just as well have stayed in India because I had no freedom. I'm a strong headed woman and slowly I came to realise that a proper life was being denied me. For two years, he never taught me anything. I didn't have any money, I had no friends of my own, I couldn't drive, I didn't even know how to use an ATM,' Ritu said.

In 2003, Ritu fell pregnant with her son Amal, now 14. As her marriage disintegrated, Ritu's life continued to spiral into a morass of fear and depression.

'I was always scared when he came home from work every day. There was never any physical violence but there was emotional, psychological and financial abuse. He would tell me I was good for nothing. "I don't know why I married you — it was the worst decision of my life," he said. I had no one to turn to. I knew no one. The emotional abuse became so bad that I would sit and cry in the house. My husband never cared about me. All he wanted was food on the table on time — but even that was never cooked properly or to his liking. Thankfully my mum was there for me — she had arrived two days before Amal was born,' she said.

At that point, Ritu realised she wanted her husband out of her life but she had no job, no money and a newborn baby.

'I decided I would bear one more year of emotional torture for the sake of my son and from that moment I started planning my escape.'

Ritu started looking for help, calling from pay phones so her husband wouldn't see the numbers she was dialling.

'Somehow I knew there would be a future for me and my son but my eyes had been opened to the fact that I could not live for long in the situation I was in,' she said.

Ritu met a single mum who worked for Centrelink and was given advice and guided through her predicament. She started planning for her and her son's future.

'My situation and my determination to escape it made me the woman I am today. I wanted to prove to myself that I could do it. And as I talked to people, I realised there was help available. Even if I was on the street, I knew that in Australia the government and other agencies would help me,' Ritu said.

With her plan in place, Ritu finally decided it was time to strike out on her own.

'She called a friend who came in her car. They loaded as many of her belongings as they we could fit in the car and drove away.

'I remember saying to him in my mind at that time "I will never again have you in my life",' she said.

Ritu was never allowed her own money but she put together an escape fund by collecting spare change left around the house. After a year she had the princely sum of $20 in a bank account she had secretly established.

'I collected five cent pieces from the floor and spare change so that I would have some money that I could call my own. It was only $20 but it was mine. I watched closely so that I could learn how to do things — how to operate in Australia. I watched how he made withdrawals from an ATM and I watched him talk to people in shops and behind counters,' she said.

Ritu spent three months in a women's refuge. She was helped by social workers from her local council to access Centrelink benefits and ultimately find her own accommodation.

'When we moved in we literally had nothing. My son and I slept on the floor but it was wonderful to have our own home.'

In 2005 Ritu secured her first job in Australia helping to run a school canteen as part of a social enterprise set up by settlement agency AMES. Through AMES she completed food handling and hospitality courses.

'We ran the canteen for three years and I was getting paid. Apart from the birth of my son, it was the best moment of my life,' Ritu said. 'I wanted to improve myself and meet more people so I agreed to speak about my experiences as a migrant woman. I was trembling before I spoke but I felt I needed to tell my story.'

Ritu's confidence grew as she made connections in her community and through childcare and women's groups. She moved on from the canteen to a job as a teller with the ANZ Bank and then as an employment consultant. But as a single mother she said she has found it difficult to gain acceptance in the Indian community.

Her trials have extended beyond an abusive marriage. In 2011 she hurt her back in a car accident and was forced to leave her bank job and last year she beat breast cancer.

'Things have slowly changed for me. There have been challenges and difficulties but when I look at where I am now compared to the worst days during my marriage I'm happy and I feel I have achieved a lot. And I'm very grateful for all the people who have helped me along the way. I am very grateful to a few people especially; Amara Hamid, a social worker with Kingston Council, Nada Mochevic who worked for AMES and helped me get my first job and Melba Marginson, the director of the Victorian Immigrant and Refugee Women's Coalition,' Ritu said.

In 2012 Ritu began working at the Hard Loch Café, in the picturesque Gippsland village of Loch and for a time owned the business. Two months after taking on her café, Ritu was diagnosed with breast cancer. She spent ten days in hospital and endured a year of chemotherapy. Two weeks after being released from hospital, she was back running her business. She was recently given a clean bill of health.

'Since the day I arrived in Australia, I haven't stopped. I've done whatever it has taken to get to where I am now,' she said.

But wanting to spend more time with her son, she now works as a teacher's aide.

'I'm blessed to be in this country and I could never have had this life in India. This country has allowed me to become what I always wanted to be. It has been an incredible journey for me in Australia for the past 15 years,' she said.

Ritu says that religion has helped her through successive ordeals in her life. A Hindu, she had limited opportunities to visit temples but found solace in the idea that there is one supreme creator and protector.

'To me there is one almighty God no matter what your religion so I would go and sit outside churches and pray to God and to Jesus for help — even as a Hindu. I believed Jesus was there to help me and when I prayed, channels opened up for me and people started coming into my life,' Ritu said.

Twelve years on from the start of her life in Australia, Ritu has some trenchant advice for other women trapped in abusive relationships.

'I would say to women: don't succumb to the situation — it does not have to be like this. You have the right to your individuality, you have right to live and there is help out there. If there is one thing I have learned it is that you do not need to suffer. And, the quicker you make the decision to get out, the better. Take hold of the opportunities that come your way and never give up your dreams and hopes. If you have the will and determination, you will achieve your dreams as I have.'

CHAPTER 40
MUMS ON A MISSION TO HELP

On a weekday afternoon in a warehouse in the backstreets of St Kilda a sophisticated logistics operation is underway. There are goods packaged according to use and customer profile, there are stock codes on every item in store and there are carefully arranged dispatch schedules. A purpose-built app keeps track of what material goes where and to whom while collecting data on customers and delivery agents.

But this is not the transport hub of a national retail giant distributing expensive, fast moving consumer goods that most of us could easily live without. This is the home of St Kilda Mums, a not-for-profit group run largely by volunteers, which donates prams, cots, car seats and just about everything else needed to care for young children to disadvantaged families.

St Kilda Mums has been operating for nine years; initially from the veranda at co-founder Jessica Macpherson's suburban home and then at a donated garage in Elwood.

'We started out helping one maternal health nurse trying to repurpose some of the things we had — so it was a tiny grass roots thing,' Jessica says.

In 2012 the group moved into a medium-sized warehouse in St Kilda; the space is organised with military precision with separate areas for each type and material and a large table used for sorting and bundling clothes and bedding.

Last year St Kilda Mums helped 13,510 disadvantaged babies and children, including in many refugee and asylum seeker households. More than 40,000 items were given out amounting to $5.2 million worth of material aid, using second hand valuations. The organisation supplies 280 social service organisations and local councils and has more than doubled its reach and impact each year of its existence. All of the clothing, blankets, toys and other items are sorted into gender-specific packs, while prams, cots and car seats are washed, repaired and safety-checked.

'Our model is based around working with social workers who come and pick up goods they need for their clients,' Jessica says. 'A social worker will call us and request some items. We package them up and have them ready and waiting for pick-up; that way no one wastes a journey and we can turn around the pick-ups very quickly.'

Run by a board of five mothers and a growing team of volunteers, St Kilda Mums has helped disadvantaged Melbourne families, from refugees and asylum seekers to women escaping violence and those simply unable to afford the baby basics.

'We concentrate on collecting stuff that will prepare a family to welcome a newborn baby home from hospital,' Jessica says. 'You may be only donating some clothing or a baby bath, but when that's put together with 10 or 20 other people's donations, suddenly you have everything that a new mum needs.'

With charities not accepting prams, car seats, cots or other nursery equipment due to safety concerns, the women realised there was no place for people wanting to donate nursery gear. 'So we stepped in to fill the gap,' Jessica says.

It is obvious listening to Jess and her volunteers that St Kilda Mums is much more than just a logistics operation. There is an obvious bond between the women — mostly mums themselves — and the people who donate pre-loved baby goods.

'I think we've tapped into something very strong. A lot of the clothes we receive have special memories attached to them for the donors — so it's beautiful they are able to give it to someone else who needs it and will really appreciate it,' Jessica says. 'We take a lot of pride in putting the clothing bags together with beautiful things, everything a mum would need from birth to about one year. We want the mums opening up those bags to feel that they are getting a gift of good quality stuff.'

St Kilda Mums also harnesses the power of social networking, using Facebook to mobilise and communicate with thousands of supporters. Much of its communication is done online, with people responding to posts requesting anything from working-bee helpers or specific clothing to the rescue of a discarded pram spotted on a suburban street.

Two like-minded groups of mums have established similar efforts in Geelong and Ballarat. Meanwhile, St Kilda Mums is helping the mother of newborn triplets in Canberra. And in 2015 the group won the state's top honour in the Victorian Premier's Sustainability Awards — the Premier's Recognition Award — for its work in recycling, reusing and re-homing baby's and children's gear.

Jessica says St Kilda Mums has been supporting some very vulnerable families with complex needs through the families' case workers and also rising numbers of teenage mums. In her experience homelessness and family violence seem to be increasing issues in families with young children getting into difficulties.

'We all know it can be an intense time when you bring home a newborn baby but is even more difficult to cope when you have no family support and a lack of material resources,' she said.

Standing in a sea of strollers and against a backdrop of bundled up clothes and toys, Jessica tells her 'half-pram story'.

'It's amazing the number of times someone will donate half a pram — which is obviously useless. But then someone else will quite coincidentally and separately donate the other half of the same type of pram — and we put them together and we have a pram to give someone. These things just shouldn't happen but they do and what that tells me is that we are doing something good and right,' she said.

CHAPTER 41
THE RUG MAKER'S JOURNEY

Najaf Mazari says that there are very few Afghans who can remember a time when there was not fighting. Before ISIS there was Al Queda and before that was the Taliban. Before the Taliban there were the Russians and the Mujahideen. And for centuries before there were the colonial and tribal conflicts.

The Afghan refugee and author of the best-selling memoir *The Rugmaker of Mazar-e-Sharif* came to Australia in an asylum seeker boat in 2001 and has rebuilt his life in Melbourne. He fled the conflict between the Taliban, dominated by a Pashtun majority, and the Hazaras, a long oppressed Shiite minority. The war in his homeland provided the soundtrack and the backdrop of the religious and ethnic conflict that dominated most of his early life. It claimed the lives of his two brothers, almost made his family destitute and finally forced him to give up everything he held dear.

'I personally believe the war in Afghanistan is the result of proxy forces from outside trying to have influence… and it's still going on. But when I was in Afghanistan I didn't know that,' Najaf said. 'I didn't know the Mujahideen were backed by the US against the communist government which was backed by the Russians — even the Mujahideen didn't know.'

Najaf says the prospects for peace in Afghanistan are not good.

'Now you have players in the west still involved but there are also forces like Pakistan and Iran,' he said. 'Ten years is nothing in Afghanistan, even a hundred years is not a long time. There are not many Afghans who can remember a time when there was no fighting.'

Between 1995 and 2000 the Taliban ruled Afghanistan with an iron fist. Claiming to be restoring peace and enforcing Sharia law, the Taliban banned everything from music to clean-shaven men. They closed schools, prevented girls from gaining an education and singled out the Hazaras for persecution.

In his book Najaf tells how the Taliban raided his home city of Mazar-e-Sharif, shooting young Hazara men on the spot. His brother and mentor Gorg Ali was killed in the fighting and his death saw the family's fortunes take a turn for the worse.

The Hazaras were expelled from Mazar-e-Sharif but Najaf refused to leave and was forced into hiding. It was his brother Gorg Ali who encouraged him to learn the skill of weaving rugs.

'I learned waving as a child. In Afghanistan there are two types of education. If you can afford it there is school, but it you can't there is learning a skill,' Najaf said. 'My brother taught me and he kept me away from the fighting and the politics. He was the one who pushed me into learning the skill of weaving. I have often thought of putting on my business card "we love rugs not war". A rug means you can enjoy the beauty of a house. I think of this when I see people destroying houses in my country. And if you have a skill you can use it anywhere.'

During the time of the Taliban Najaf was beaten, flogged and threatened with being burned alive. He also once hid in cupboard for 12 days evading capture — and worse — at the hands the Taliban.

He says that rather than become embittered, his faith in the goodness of God was strengthened during his ordeals.

Once, when his leg was injured in a rocket attack and he was bedridden for weeks, he says he was forced to think about his life and its challenges.

'I attempted to profit from this period of being bedridden by thinking of such matters of importance. I knew that I had to be strong in my body and my mind for whatever is to happen,' Najaf said.

And he says that weaving carpets gave him time to think about the prospect of a better life; a life filled with hope and prosperity.

'It was this double weaving in my mind and on the loom, that kept my spirits high, when the Mujahideen chased me and the communists chased me and the war went on and on and the jets roared overhead,' Najaf said.

He says he simply refused to give in to the Taliban. And because of his resilience, it was decided by his family that he should be the one to make a perilous journey to safety.

'My family said that leaving Afghanistan, even illegally, was my best chance of survival,' Najaf said. 'The trip was risky but life in Afghanistan was a risk. Things were already scary. If you stayed your life was in danger; if you left your life was in danger. Nothing is easy. It is very painful to have to leave your country and to leave you family.'

After a perilous journey through Pakistan, Indonesia and by boat to Australia, Najaf ended up in immigration detention. He says that many of his follow asylum seekers at the Woomera Detention Centre lived in constant fear of being deported back to the countries they had fled.

'The most difficult thing about detention is not knowing your future. Waiting is difficult and people get depressed,' Najaf said.

After being released from detention, Najaf became an Australian citizen and was joined by his wife and daughter. He has started an Afghan rug retail business in Melbourne, he is on the public speaking circuit and has written two books; *The Rugmaker of Mazar-e-Sharif* and *The Honey Thief.*

The first of these is now the subject of a movie project to be directed by Anthony LaPaglia. And the earnings from the book have funded an ambulance for his village.

'If I can save one life a year, I believe I have done my job,' Najaf said.

He says he is fortunate to have found a new life in Australia, which has provided his family with a bright future. But Najaf says not all newcomers to this country are given a fair go.

'Sometimes when people come to Australia, especially those who come by boat they have skills,' he said. 'But some employers won't give them a chance. When I first arrived, I went to a carpet factory to look for a job and I saw they were using "finishing machine" which evens out the length of the pile. It takes six months to master this machine and I had used the machine at home in Afghanistan. But the owner wouldn't let me show him I could do the work because he was worried I would ruin his carpets — which is easy to do with this machine. But I convinced him to let me use it on a small piece of rug. When he saw me use the machine he offered me a permanent job. I think businesses and employers in Australia could benefit from using the skills refugees and newcomers bring with them.'

He says he is 'blessed' to have a life in Australia.

'I run a small business which is tough, it's not easy,' Najaf said. 'But coming to Australia has opened my eyes about the world. And when I am speaking publicly I try to tell people what is going on in Afghanistan. Australia is a fortunate country. It has been fortunate for me and it meant that I wrote two books. And through those I was able to get out a message of peace,' Najaf said.

Najaf's 18-year-old daughter Maria has followed in her father's footsteps. She is studying textile design and interior decorating at RMIT.

'I didn't push her into it. I told her "study what you love" but she went ahead anyway,' he said.

Asked about what he has learned on his journey as a refugee, Najaf tells a story that he says sums up his attitude to life.

'To me justice and fairness are important. As a Hazara I understand what it is to be a minority, to be persecuted and to be targeted. When I was on the boat coming to Australia, I was cooking for 96 people. We only had a little rice and potato but I made sure the women and children were fed first. Then I made sure the minority people on the boat were fed and then I fed my own people. The Hazara men were served last. I think this was important. It was saying to people you are valued, you are part of this united group and we are together on this journey.'

CHAPTER 42
OF COWS, WOMEN AND WAR
– A REFUGEE'S STORY

Multi-talented South Sudanese singer Ajak Kwai came to Australia as a refugee fleeing the brutal and interminable civil war in her homeland. Having re-established her life here, Ajak is sharing through her music her own story and the rich culture of her people.

As a Dinka woman, Ajak has used singing and storytelling to help maintain her connection to her people and their cultural traditions as well as assuaging the trials and trauma of being a refugee forced to flee everything she held dear.

Ajak says that as a child she had a speech impediment and avoided talking. But her memory and natural musical talent made her the songwoman of her village and a custodian of her people's stories.

But when war broke out, her fiancé was forced to join the military and was killed. Subsequently, she lost her father, two brothers, two nephews and several cousins and her village was attacked and razed by rival militia.

'The militia came to my home town and killed everyone,' she said. 'Some people died of hunger because they looted the town, people were hiding in the bush, and they had no food.'

Luckily for Ajak, she had already fled to the city with her uncle.

'My village has gone. There is nothing there to go back to,' Ajak said.

Despite the devastation, Dinka culture remains a central pillar of Ajak's life.

'I come from the Sudan. My culture as a Dinka person is very unique. We are nomads, very strong-minded people and sometimes people don't like us,' she said. 'In Sudan, we did pay a very huge price because of the war which was absolutely devastating. My country South Sudan was absolutely devastated by the war. Many people were killed or forced to flee their homes. But we still hold our pride. People become miserable, people have lost their homes, they've lost their animals.'

But Ajak has found solace in music at the most difficult times in her life.

'Music helped me a lot in my life,' she said. 'My mum died when I was quite young. My father had another wife, so I did not really live with my father for a long time. I was withdrawn and I did not talk very much. When I became a refugee, music helped a lot because I would write a lot of poems and sing. Singing and music gave me hope and an outlet for my feelings. We were refugees in Cairo for a long time, for eight years. It's a long time to be staying, doing nothing. The music, the singing, the writing it really helped me in my journey from the Sudan to here.'

Ajak was almost lost to Australia as many of her fellow South Sudanese refugees were drawn to attempt to get to the US. At first suspicious of Australia's colonial past, she says she has felt welcome here since arriving in 2001.

'The group of people I was with wanted to go to America and I was going to go with them. And at the time we heard that Australia had killed its black people a long time ago and that they don't like black people at all. I went to the Australian embassy in Cairo and we met young Australian people at the embassy and they were very good looking young people but me and my cousin — we joked "Oh my god, they so look ugly because they are so mean",' she laughs.

Ajak says she sees similarities between African and Australian Indigenous cultures and is moved by the plight of some aboriginal communities.

'I travelled around Australia in 2011 playing at festivals and I heard a lot of Indigenous musicians and met the people in communities,' she said. 'Actually, the indigenous cultures here are very similar to our African culture. The stories are similar you know. I saw people sitting under the trees and that made me think about home. And that's how I came to write my stories because I could see the pain in the eyes of these people. They were sitting there. There are no jobs and they are struggling. But these are beautiful welcoming people. So, to be able to see them like that it reminded me of the sadness I felt at home during the war. And to see some of problems aboriginal people have is so sad because there is no war here. It's good to know where people come from. It's good to know about what it's like for other people in their lives. I'm very proud of my people because I think they are very good people and the novelty of the Dinka people, I love that. And everyone in South Sudan, I feel for them.'

Ajak was originally settled in Tasmania but moved to Melbourne in 2007, drawn by the city's vibrant music scene. She has performed constantly since them and has been a regular at the WOMADelaide festivals in recent years.

Her 'Of Cows, Women and War' theatre show, was released as an album in February 2016, and is a rich mixture of African-soul melodies and tells of her extraordinary journey from being exiled from her home, to gospel singing in Cairo and starting afresh in Melbourne.

CHAPTER 43
REFUGEE DOCTOR WANTS TO CONTRIBUTE

As a doctor working in Iraq during the conflict there, Asseel Yako saved hundreds of lives. His daily work was tending to battlefield wounds suffered by soldiers or militia members fighting ISIS or patching up women and children horrifically injured in explosions or gunfire.

He has studied and worked as a doctor for almost twenty years and here in Australia he has set out on a path to resume his career.

For Asseel, in his home town of Qaraqosh even travelling to work at the city's hospital was perilous.

'It was dangerous simply getting to work. There were bombs, kidnappings and people were killed on the street,' Asseel said. 'A friend of ours — a surgeon — just disappeared one day.'

Asseel loved his work as a doctor in Qaraqosh — a largely Assyrian city in northern Iraq — and now living in Australia as a refugee he wants to work and contribute to give back to the country that afforded his family sanctuary.

'Inside the town things were dangerous but OK for a while. We had different people coming from other parts of Iraq to the hospital in the town,' Asseel said. 'When the security forces were present, everything was fine but when they left after ISIS came it became ever dangerous.'

Asseel took his family away from Qaraqosh and eventually to Jordon in August 2014.

'My wife was pregnant and about to go into labour. We moved to Erbil — a ten-hour road trip — and after a week my wife gave birth to our son Darwin,' he said.

The family stayed in Erbil until February 2015 when they moved to Jordan.

'We rented an apartment there and I worked as a volunteer in a refugee camp for Syrians and Iraqis because I was not allowed to work,' Asseel said. 'We lived in a poor area in the town but even there rents were very high and life was difficult. After one year our visa application was accepted and we moved here to Australia. We arrived in February and lived at first in Werribee then we moved here to St Albans to be closer to some relatives who are helping us.'

As members of a Christian minority in Iraq they were subject to repression.

'But things were quiet until 2014 when ISIS invaded Iraq — they are an aggressive and bloody militia,' Asseel said. 'We could not stay in our town because we knew they would kill us. We saw what happened to the Yazidis… they took the women, killed the men and enslaved the boys. In our town 100,000 people fled their homes.'

Asseel studied medicine for five years and worked as a doctor for more than a decade.

'I am doctor. It is all I know. I saved a lot of lives in Iraq. It is what I was born to do,' he said. 'When we arrived in Australia we received a lot of help regarding our general life but not much support in terms of resuming my medical career. I still need a lot of help in finding my pathway. It looks like it will take about five years and a lot of money to get qualified and to pass the steps that mean I can work as a doctor.'

The Occupational English Test he had to pass required a very high standard of English. Five small errors, including using the wrong tense when writing a verb, could have meant failure. Asseel also faced an interview with the Australia College of Physicians and was approved to go ahead and find a job and then complete a four-year medical course.

He has recently secured a two-year traineeship at Warragul Hospital. If he had not found the job, his approval would have lapsed after a year and he would have had to start all over again.

The interview cost him $6,000, which was not refundable if he had not passed. Added to this is the $10,000 fee the Australian Medical Council charged to verify his qualifications and documents before he could even start the process.

Asseel says his family lived for two years as internally displaced persons (IDPs) in Iraq and received no support from anyone, including the Iraqi government.

'Since we arrived in Australia, we have received a lot of help,' he said. 'When we arrived my daughter Roxanne had pneumonia and was in hospital seriously ill for a week. In the aeroplane coming here there was someone who was obviously sick, he was coughing all the time. I think that is how Roxanne got sick. There are a lot of people from Qaraqosh here. Most are working or studying English. All of them are fine.'

Asseel said he was working hard to rebuild his life in Australia.

'I lost everything: my job, my house and the good life I was leading. I had just finished years of studying and now I have to start all over again,' he said.

But Asseel is grateful that his family is safe.

'I want to thank the Australian Government for what it has done for us. At the time when we were in desperate need, no one else — except maybe Canada — was accepting us,' he said.

Asseel has recently secured a training residency in a hospital in country Victoria.

'I am looking forward to restarting my career in Australia and contributing to this country by working as a doctor,' Asseel said.

CHAPTER 44
REFUGEE'S LONG, DIFFICULT JOURNEY ENDS IN MELBOURNE

Afghan refugee Mirwais Janbaz vividly remembers his first brush with death. As a seven-year-old he was sent by his family to buy bread at a shop just 100 metres from his home.

'I was just ten metres from the bread shop when suddenly it was hit by a rocket. The shop was destroyed and everyone inside was killed,' Mirwais said. 'I jumped into a small stream that ran past the bakery and I thought I would die. After a time, I looked up and there was just blood and smoke everywhere. I ran home and my uncle had run over to the shop to find me. When I got home my family didn't recognise me because my clothes and my face were so dirty. When my uncle got home, he said everyone in the bakery had been killed. It was a very bad time.

This seminal moment in Mirwais' life came in the early 1990s as fighting raged between rival Mujahideen groups for control of the Afghan capital of Kabul in the wake of the power vacuum created by the Russian withdrawal. The fighting started in April 1992 and involved six rival armed groups led by warlords. Over the course of the year hundreds of rockets hit Kabul and thousands, mostly civilians, were killed and around half a million people fled the city.

In 1993, the rival militia factions continued their fight over Kabul and several cease-fires and peace accords failed.

By 1995 the fighting, now across all of Afghanistan, had been distilled into conflict between four factions: Burhanuddin Rabbani's 'interim government'; the Taliban; the forces of former Afghan communist general Abdul Rashid Dostum; and the anti-Soviet Hizb-e Wahdat group.

The byzantine web of intrigue and violence was the backdrop to Mirwais' early childhood.

Now rebuilding his life from his new home in Melbourne's south-east, Mirwais has told of his strife-wracked life journey.

'I was a child living in Kabul during the civil war and I remember friends and neighbours being killed,' he said. 'Also, my uncle, my father's brother was killed in the war. He was a teacher and he ran a real estate business. A rocket came and hit his shop and he was injured. He lost part of both his legs and he died six months later. During the civil war we were stuck inside Kabul unable to leave. There was fighting everywhere and there was no way to get out. Rockets and bombs were being fired all the time and I lost friends and neighbours whose homes were hit. As kids we would sometimes count the numbers of rockets we could hear.'

When the Taliban eventually seized control of Kabul, Mirwais' family thought that, despite the regime's repressive policies, there at least would be peace. But when one day the Taliban arrived wanting to take one of Mirwais' siblings away and force them into the service of regime, his father decided it was time to flee.

'That evening my father took us to the house of one of his friends and the next day, early in the morning, we left for Pakistan,' Mirwais said.

The family crossed in Pakistan at the Torkham Border, a busy crossing spot in Nangarhar Province.

'As we crossed the border some soldiers asked for money and they beat me when I didn't have any,' Mirwais said.

They settled in Islamabad where Mirwais' aunt already lived and Mirwais attended refugee schools funded by the UN where he excelled in drawing, painting and calligraphy. But going on to further study was difficult as Afghan refugees in Pakistan are not afforded official status or ID documents.

'After high school, it took me two years to get the documents I needed to get to university to study journalism and mass communications,' Mirwais said. 'Successive governments in Pakistan have made their own laws about refugees so it is very difficult to know where you stand.'

Mirwais and his family spent 20 years living in limbo in Pakistan not knowing what the future held or whether they would be forced to return to their war-torn homeland. To make a living, Mirwais took painting and drawing commissions from people, including embassy staff, who liked his artworks. He also worked on call as an interpreter for the UN's migration agency, the IOM, as a speaker of six languages.

But it was in Islamabad where tragedy struck the family. In 2001 his older brother Waleed was electrocuted because of poor wiring in the apartment they rented. Waleed was just 22 years old and the tragic incident caused, and is still causing, a great deal of grief for Mirwais and his family, who say the incident was never investigated by the authorities.

Ironically, Mirwais — through his work with IOM — also helped deliver the Australian government's orientation session for refugees granted visas to come here.

'Because of this, I knew a lot about Australia before I came here. I even met an Afghan lady on train who told me that she had met in Pakistan when I had done an orientation session,' Mirwais said.

He also worked for a time at the Brazilian embassy where he learned about the Brazilian martial art Capoeira. Mirwais took to the sport and won a scholarship for a study tour to Brazil. He has since become an instructor.

'I love the philosophy of Capoeira. It is a fighting sport but really it is about community, humanity, self-respect and confidence,' he said.

In Pakistan he taught the sport to young refugees to give them confidence and an outlet to their fears and frustrations.

Mirwais arrived in Melbourne six months after his parents and brother.

'Arriving in Australia was a life changing moment for me,' he said. 'In Pakistan I had no identity. We were scared of the police and they would take money from us with guns. We weren't allowed to work or open a bank account. The police pick on refugees and ask for money. People who can't pay or don't know anyone are put in jail. When I arrived in Melbourne, there was a woman in uniform (border force official) who welcomed me to Australia in a very kind way. That was the best moment.'

Mirwais says he is now keen to find a job.

'In the short term, I want to find work and I will learn some new skills if I need to. I don't want to take money from the government. I am very grateful to the Australian government and the Australian people and I want to pay them back for giving me a safe place to live,' he said. 'But I also plan to continue my studies and with my art and with Capoeira. That is my future plan.'

CHAPTER 45
STUDYING AND STRIVING IN WARTIME – A REFUGEE'S STORY

Studying by candlelight in the bowels of an ancient convent as a bloody civil war raged around her, Jamila Alarkan stuck doggedly to her dream of becoming an engineer. The Syrian refugee endured the effects of war, sickness and physical injury to pursue an education and the chance of a bright future. Amid some of the fiercest fighting of the Syrian conflict and the destruction of the ancient city of Aleppo and with friends and classmates being killed at random, Jamila stuck to her studies — not knowing if she would ever have a chance to use the knowledge she was acquiring.

For five years she battled the fallout from the conflict that has devastated her homeland, eventually graduating with a degree in mechanical engineering. But with Syria in ruins and little chance of work, she and her husband Tony took the gamble of their lives and left their families and everything and everyone they had known and loved in search of a future. Now, settled safely in Melbourne, they have started down a pathway to resurrect their professional careers in Australia.

'Engineering has been my passion for as long as I can remember. My hero is my sister Dahlia who is 10 years older than me and an engineer,' she said. 'I've always loved mathematics and science and when Dahlia studied engineering, I loved the drawings she used in her course. I've always enjoyed building things and making things work and I really love problem solving and finding solutions, so I knew I wanted to be an engineer when I grew up.'

In 2010, Jamila, whose family lived in Tartus on Syria's Mediterranean coast, was accepted into university in the ancient city of Aleppo, in the country's north, and began her engineering studies.

'It was an exciting year and I finished my first year with very good marks. This first year was very happy,' she said. 'All my subjects were available and I was learning English and we lived a normal and safe life. At that time, life in Syria was good. Before the war we had a perfect life. Before the war my parents worked in farms and my father worked two jobs so that they could secure all that we needed during our studies at school and at university. They struggled to give us a lovely childhood and a good education. Back then, our relationships with other communities were good and we had a lot of friends from different sects. We lived in one society and all studied together in one school or university. But during my second year at university, the war began in many parts of Syria and it finally reached Aleppo. Despite this terrible situation, I finished my second year and passed all my subjects.'

But the situation took a turn for the worse for Jamila and most other Syrians in 2012. The war escalated significantly and Aleppo was besieged — cut off from the rest of Syria — as the fighting intensified.

'There was no way that the city of Aleppo could be reached from outside, so I could not go back to the university for my third year,' Jamila said. 'I was able to register at another university in a less dangerous city, Homs, 200 kilometres to the south, but I could not study all the basic third year engineering subjects because this university did not offer the same specialisations. I went back home empty handed to my family in Tartus. I was heartbroken because I could not complete my studies. My university was besieged by war, all my dreams to become an engineer crashed and the war was spreading all over Syria. The situation was serious and getting even worse.'

She says she lost her desire for life and was depressed about the situation. She lost her appetite and suffered severe anaemia, shortness of breath and sleeplessness.

'After a few months, a road was opened to Aleppo. This was not really safe but it was the only way I could get back to my university in that city. I made my decision to complete my studies no matter what. So, I decided to attempt to reach Aleppo via this road. My family were opposed my decision as they feared for my life. That period was one of the worst I've ever experienced but despite their concerns and the dangers, I didn't change my mind.'

Jamila took a dangerous 12-hour bus ride into Aleppo and back for her studies.

As a Christian, she lived in a convent near the university, along with other students and the nuns.

'We were subjected constantly to conditions of war such as lack of water, electricity, food and safety,' Jamila said. 'The city was under siege and sometimes I was disconnected from my family for weeks as with no electricity, I couldn't charge my phone. Most nights we slept in the shelter of the convent because of missiles and explosions. Many of my friends died in this war. And one of the nuns who sheltered us died in a bombing incident near where I was sleeping in the convent. One time I was hit in the leg and had to go to hospital for one week. I was also poisoned several times due to the remnants of war — our water and food were contaminated by chemicals and the terrorists threw bodies into the city's water supply from where we obtained our drinking water.'

Despite the conflict and the dangers and privations it brought, Jamila managed to graduate after the five years of study.

She told how she studied by candlelight for hours each night in the convent.

'These were difficult times and it's very hard to remember how we all survived all this terror,' Jamila said. 'I came so close several times to being seriously injured — or worse. But, in spite of all these difficulties, it was at this time that I met my husband Tony. We met each other in Homs when a friend introduced us and we married in 2017. Tony's life was also very difficult and he has his own stories about that war. He studied electrical engineering and after he graduated, he studied for his Masters in Alternative Energies.'

The couple built a house in Homs to live in after they were married but this was destroyed by missiles.

'We had no choice as we could no longer live there,' Jamila said. 'We were faced with the situation of having no work, no home, no safety and no future in this endless and horrible war. So, we decided to leave our families and our beloved country to flee to a safe place so we travelled to another country, Iraq, to apply for humanitarian visas for Australia.'

The couple waited in Iraq for eight months before being granted visas.

'We were very lucky that our request was accepted and we were able to come to Australia,' Jamila said.

Tony also had a difficult time during the conflict.

'I grew up in Homs. I graduated in electrical engineering at the university there in 2011,' Tony said. 'But Homs was where the war first began. When it started we went to our home town in the countryside near Homs and stayed there a year. After a year I was able to start a Masters Degree at Homs. I couldn't travel there in the interim because of the fighting.

'At the same time, I started work at an oil refinery in the city. The refinery was a strategic place for Syria — one of only two in the country — so it was attacked by ISIS. ISIS shelled the refinery and some days we could not go there — but sometimes we had to go to keep the place running. There were a lot of factories and companies in Syria before the war — especially in Aleppo. But they were destroyed by ISIS, who also took a lot of the equipment out of the country. But I think Syria can recover economically in time.'

The couple now live in Melbourne's north. They speak to their families in Syria each day.

'We miss them so much but we are safe and we have many friends here now,' Jamila said.

Jamila and Tony are studying English at AMES Australia and are preparing for the IELTS test, which is part of the process of having their professional qualifications recognised. They both hope to soon launch the careers in Australia as engineers.

'We can't wait to start our professional lives here in Melbourne, to contribute at last and to be part of our new society,' Jamila said.

CHAPTER 46
VOYAGE TO FREEDOM

'Mine is a very sad story,' says Hao Quach.

Sitting outside a café in Footscray almost forty years since he fled his homeland, the former Vietnamese refugee is reflecting on his life as a naval officer, labour camp prisoner and boat person forced to flee everything he had known and loved. But he says the sadness has been tempered over the years by the lives his children have been able to build in Australia.

After surviving a brutal war, four years in a gulag, a perilous journey though pirate-infested seas and thirty years of back-breaking factory work, Hao's says his greatest achievement are his three sons.

One son Nam Hoang, sitting beside him in the café, is an engineer working in renewable energy and recently was the Mayor of Footscray. Another son is a teacher and farmer who is active in refugee support groups and the other runs his own catering business.

Echoing a familiar migrant sentiment, Hao says that since leaving Vietnam his life has been all about his sons. He says his own early life was uneventful. But like millions of others, it was completely and irreversibly changed by the advent of the Vietnam War.

'Growing up I had a normal life, my parents ran a business. School was free and I loved learning,' he says. 'But I finished high school in 1968 just after the Tet Offensive.'

The offensive was a campaign of surprise attacks by the North Vietnamese Army and Viet Cong guerillas against military and civilian command and control centres throughout South Vietnam timed to coincide with the Vietnamese New Year, or Tet, holiday.

'This was a massive attack that really brought the war into people's lives and woke up the country. After Tet the war intensified,' Hao said. 'All boys of military age had to go into the services. So, I joined the navy.'

Hao was sent to study navigation a ship handling at the US Navy's Naval War College at Newport, Rhode Island, and then served aboard a warship patrolling coastal waters off South Vietnam for five years. The patrols were aimed stopping the North Vietnamese delivering weapons to the Viet Cong guerrillas operating in the south. They were so successful that the North Vietnamese sought another way to move arms. This led to the creation of the infamous Ho Chi Minh trail — a series of jungle paths that wound through Laos and Cambodia along which the North Vietnamese supplied arms to the Viet Cong in the south.

'We patrolled from the 17th parallel south to the Gulf of Thailand,' Hao said.

In 1975 he went back to naval college in Saigon as the war took a turn for the worse.

'It was a terrible time, very hard. The communists were closing in and everyone was afraid for the future,' Hao said.

When the communists took control Hao, along with thousands of other South Vietnamese servicemen, officials and business people was sent to a 're-education camp'.

'This was really a forced labour camp. They didn't kill you with a gun or a knife but they killed you in a different way,' Hao said. 'We were made to do hard labour from early in the morning until late at night. A lot of former South Vietnamese soldiers died in that camp.'

Hao spent four interminable years in the camp. 'I was lucky. Some people spent decades in these camps. They were designed to break your will,' he said.

When he was in the camp, Hao's wife Le-Ha was virtually a single mother left to bring up the couple's first son Nam Do.

While most South Vietnamese lost their jobs as socialism and wealth redistribution was imposed on the south, because the communists needed to keep the banking system operating Le-Ha kept her job working in a bank. But the communists confiscated most of her property and even commandeered her house while Hao was in prison.

Upon his release from the labour camp Hao knew immediately he could not remain in his homeland. 'I knew I could not live in Vietnam anymore. I was thinking not about me but about my children and their futures. There would be nothing for them in Vietnam,' he said.

Some local businessmen had bought a boat and were preparing to leave but they had no one who could navigate the vessel, Hao said.

'When I got out of the camp they asked me to do it,' he said. 'But what they had bought was basically a river boat so we had to make it seaworthy. We changed the shape of the boat and strengthened it to suit the high seas. The work took quite a while. But finally we were ready and we set sail early on the morning of 1 April 1979.'

Twenty miles off the coast on the first morning they were attacked by Thai pirates who would continue to raid and harass them for six consecutive days.

'They took everything — money, gold earrings, everything we had,' Hao said.

On the sixth day the pirates returned and this time started to separate the men and women on the boat.

'We were terrified about what they were planning to do but luckily a merchant ship passing by saw what was happening and came to help us. This made the pirates run away,' he said.

Hao says the ordeal may have prompted his pregnant wife to go into labour. Soon after he delivered his second son Nam Ha while still at sea.

'My son was born at sea on that sixth day. He had not been due for another month but as soon as he came along, I knew we had to get him and my wife to safety,' Hao said.

The plan had been to sail all the way to Australia but Hao decided to put into the Malaysian port of Kuantan.

'I had heard the Malaysians were not accepting any more refugees because the camps were full — and they were forcing boats back out to sea,' he said. 'So, I got the women and children ashore at a quiet beach and then I sailed into the port. I told the Malaysian police that the boat was sinking so they could not tow us out to sea.'

After four months in a refugee camp Hao, his wife and two sons were accepted for resettlement in Australia. At the time, then Australian Prime Minister Malcom Fraser took the politically risky approach of instituting a proactive and generous humanitarian response to the Indochinese refugee crisis. Between 1976 and 1982 nearly 70,000 Indochinese were resettled in Australia and approximately 80,000 came after via the orderly departure scheme and immigration channels established by the Fraser government. In later life, Fraser became a passionate and vociferous advocate for asylum seekers and refugees and his legacy is recognised in a mural on the wall of Footscray's Asylum Seeker Resource Centre.

'We arrived in Australia with nothing. I think I had two pairs of shorts and two shirts,' Hao said. 'But we received a lot of help from the Australian people. We were given new clothes and we stayed for two months at a migrant hostel in Altona.'

The family was sponsored to settle in Geelong and Hao began work in a rope factory. His wife worked in a shoe factory.

'For ten years I worked night shifts. I would get home and had to take the kids to school before I could sleep,' he said.

Nam Hoang, born in Australia in 1981, says that several local families helped them out.

'These families were our "Australian angels". They would take us kids to school and look after us. It was like having second mothers,' he said. 'We formed close bonds and strong connections with these families that helped us in the 1980s. For me growing up in Australia was quite normal. But on refection, if we hadn't had the support of these families it would have been much more difficult for us. Effectively we lived in a sponsored environment with second mothers and second families who helped us understand how things worked in Australia. We were very lucky to have that.'

He said his family often reflected on at their good fortune in finding safety in Australia.

'I guess the things we talk about as a family are the difficult times. Dad delivering my brother on the boat, Dad's prison experience and Mum having to carry on with no husband,' he said. 'These things make us as a family appreciate what we have and where we are. It's hard to have a bad day when you've lived through these things.'

As our conversation comes to an end, Nam Hoang reveals that his grandfather — Hao's father — was also a refugee forced to flee China after 1948 as part of the Nationalist regime defeated by Mao's communists.

'My grandfather, my father, my mother and my brothers have all been refugees,' Ham Hoang said. 'My hope is that the next generation is where that trend stops and my kids don't have to be refugees.'

CHAPTER 47
SURVIVING GENOCIDE

The 1990s gave us *Friends*, Bill Clinton, the World Wide Web, hip hop and *Seinfeld*. But it also gave us the worst genocide in Europe since the Holocaust.

The civil war in Bosnia started in 1992 when a referendum on the independence of Bosnia and Herzegovina was passed in the aftermath of the breakup of Yugoslavia. Self-proclaimed Bosnian Serb and Bosnian Croat nationalist groups opposed the move and conflict resulted. An horrific feature of the war was the siege of Sarajevo, the Bosnian capital. It was the longest siege in modern warfare and over four years the city was the scene of bitter fighting that claimed almost 14,000 lives, including those of 5,400 civilians.

Vedran Drakulic lived through the destruction of his city. He says that options were limited for men and boys living in the capital. Either you joined the army or tried to escape. If you chose to stay, you risked falling victim to the constant bombing, sniping and shell fire. Vedran says he was lucky in that he got a job with the International Committee of Red Cross. From 1992 to 1995 he worked for them — as a logistics officer, interpreter, and press officer.

These jobs meant he worked across the front lines of the war, helping injured individuals on both sides of the conflict. Even though he had the opportunity to leave earlier, Vedran chose to stay through three years of the war.

'I needed to take care of my family. While I was still in Sarajevo, I was getting a salary from the Red Cross and I could help feed and protect my family,' Vedran said. 'I always had a desire to escape, especially after my brother's death during the first few months of fighting, when he was killed by bombing as a civilian, but I couldn't leave my family.'

His brother's death was one of 100,000 recorded during the Bosnian

War. And while Vedran vowed to stay to help his family and others, it eventually got to be too much.

'I escaped thanks to my work across the front lines with the Red Cross and managed to go to Split, in Croatia, after spending three years in the war,' he said. 'By that time in 1995, I was married and my wife Anita joined me two-and-a-half months later.'

Even though fighting ended only a few months after his escape — with a NATO bombing campaign forcing Bosnian Serbs to the negotiating table where the peace agreement, the Dayton Accords, was signed in December 1995 — Vedran wanted to get as far away from Europe and the terrors of the war as possible.

'In Split, we began our process of trying to resettle. Split was sort of a "clearing station" for people trying to go somewhere else, we couldn't stay nor did we want to after what we had lived through,' Vedran said 'A lot of non-European countries were accepting refugees from the Bosnian conflict due to the world-wide media attention it was getting at the time. We applied for resettlement to Canada, America and Australia. These countries were providing Bosnian refugees proper residency conditions, whereas immigrating to somewhere in Europe meant being put behind barbed wire in compounds only to be sent back to a destroyed Bosnia after the war.'

The US was the first to accept Vedran and Anita. But, this wasn't their first choice. Australia was the nation they wanted to call home, so they waited in Split hoping to receive a letter from the Australian Embassy.

'There were two reasons we wanted Australia,' Vedran said. 'Firstly, I worked with a woman at Red Cross who was from Australia. Her father was a QC in Cairns and she said if we decided to go there he would help my wife and I. The second reason was we wanted to get as far away from the conflict in the Balkans as possible, and Australia is pretty much as far as it gets.'

Six months later the letter arrived, affording residency in Australia to Vedran and Anita under the government's humanitarian refugee resettlement program. Not wishing to spend any longer in Europe, the couple flew to Brisbane where Vedran's friend's father met them and took them to a house he owned in Rockhampton.

The move from Split, on the Adriatic Riviera to Rockhampton in Queensland was a bit of a culture shock. But the couple were grateful to be out of Europe and enjoyed every minute of their new-found freedom from war and displacement.

'We spent two to three weeks at this house in Rockhampton with Cassy the dog and a fully stocked fridge, just relaxing and drinking this thing they call beer — "Four X",' Vedran said with a smile.

After spending time unwinding in Rockhampton, the couple resettled in Brisbane where they were assessed for language and got re-involved with the Red Cross. But resettling in Brisbane wasn't easy.

'We had a huge cultural shock after coming from cities in Europe that were buzzing, full of life,' says Vedran. 'We had spent our whole life in a city environment, where it was full of life. In Brisbane, we would be walking around city at 5pm and everything was quiet.'

But reading Melbourne's *The Age* newspaper every day planted in Vedran an interest in the southern city. Fortunately, *The Age* was being shipped from Melbourne to Brisbane and arriving every Sunday morning — Vedran took a specific interest in the Melbourne-based paper's jobs section. It was while reading one of the classifieds that he noticed an advertisement for a job in Melbourne at the Australian Red Cross.

'I applied for a job in Melbourne at the Australian Red Cross and flew there to meet with the head of the Public Affairs Department, who at the time was Robyn Thompson,' Vedran said. 'While in the meeting the CEO of Red Cross came in, former politician Jim Carlton. Jim heard there was a job applicant from Bosnia, a refugee. He had visited Bosnia only a few months back and wanted to check me out. After a brief chat with me, he told Robyn to give me the job right away. From that moment on, Jim became my mentor and good friend. I didn't want to be a burden on this country. We moved to Melbourne so we could work hard and give back. We didn't want Centrelink support or any support really.'

Vedran says he is grateful to the Red Cross for the opportunities provided to him in Australia. He says he was fortunate the organisation took a risk on him by employing a person they didn't know and who had never worked in the country before.

'My story as a refugee made me want to stay working for the Red Cross. From working with them in Bosnia, it was clear they provided literally lifesaving humanitarian assistance during the conflict,' he said. 'In Yugoslavia, Red Cross was mainly known as blood service, but through the Bosnian War with Red Cross, they opened my eyes to humanitarian work and the things they do when it comes to conflict or even natural disasters, and how they help people.'

This passion and appreciation for humanitarian work is something Vedran got hooked on and rapidly became involved in — it was also a way to give back to the country who gave him and Anita a chance to start all over again.

Since arriving in Australia over 20 years ago, Vedran has committed his career to humanitarian work. From working with Red Cross, to Oxfam Australia and now as the CEO of Gandel Philanthropy. He is also a board member of refugee and migrant settlement agency AMES Australia. Because of his humble beginnings as a refugee, Vedran also works as a volunteer at AMES as he believes it is important to do something for people who are experiencing what he went through.

Vedran received the Medal of the Order of Australia (OAM) in January 2017. He described the emotions stirred up by the award as both shocking and humbling.

'I think everyone who does this line of work doesn't expect to be recognised for it, doesn't do it for the accolades,' he said.

But the more poignant aspect of receiving the award for Vedran was finding out who nominated him for such an honour.

'Jim Carlton was the one who nominated me. I found out after his death and after receiving the award. His wife told me that it was Jim who nominated me as he believed in me entirely — I was completely overcome,' he said. 'Jim was known as a "dying breed" of politicians, one who could bring Liberals and Labor together and overcome the political divide. Enough to say that at his funeral the former prime ministers John Howard and Paul Keating, as well as the former deputy prime minister Tim Fischer, were all in attendance.'

Being a refugee has come to be part of how Vedran defines himself. He recognised as much in his acceptance speech for the OAM.

'An important element for me is that I came to this country as a refugee so I felt a responsibility to dedicate the award to all the other refugees who came here and contributed to this country,' Vedran said. 'Too often we hear refugees are a burden on society, here to trick us, or be dole bludgers. I believe that by and large this is not true, I strongly believe most refugees try to make a new life and have incredible obstacles to overcome, such as learning the language and getting that first break in the workforce. And I can promise you, most of them want to give back.'

And after overcoming many obstacles himself, both emotional and physical, Vedran is doing just that.

CHAPTER 48
LONG WALK TO SAFETY – A SUDANESE REFUGEE'S JOURNEY TO MANHOOD

As a small boy Peter Kon was forced on a month-long march across rugged bushland away from his family and village. For the next 18 years a refugee camp would be his home and disease, starvation and death his constant companions. But the South Sudanese refugee refused to give up his dream of a future.

Now resettled in Australia, the 40-year-old has gained multiple tertiary qualifications and has worked in the humanitarian sector for agencies that support newly arrived refugees. He has become a leader in his community and is at the centre of grappling with issues around disengaged South Sudanese youth.

'As a young boy, I lived in a village in the countryside,' Peter said. 'It was a happy life, free of stress. We had livestock and we grew native foods in our garden. But then in 1983 war came and things changed very much for the worse.'

Sudan in the 1980s was governed by an Islamic regime based in Khartoum, in the north of the country. When Christian groups in the south formed to push for an independent nation the Khartoum government targeted them using armed militias, including the infamous Janjaweed.

'Things became very bad for us. The government in Khartoum began kidnapping young boys and pressing them into the army — some of these boys were as young as nine,' Peter said.

The story of Africa's boy soldiers has become well known, the subject of a series of books and films.

The Sudan People's Liberation Army (SPLA) formed by Christian groups in the south to oppose the Islamic government in Khartoum began rounding up young boys and taking them to Ethiopia with promises of keeping them safe from the government. Peter was one of these 'lost' boys forced to walk across rugged bushland with little food and no protection from marauding government militia or even wild animals.

'The SPLA came and said that they were taking all the boys to safety. So in 1987, I left Sudan,' Peter said. 'We walked for a month to get to Ethiopia. We walked mostly at night and we slept under trees. Sometimes there was no food and some boys had no shoes. We ate wildlife and native fruit. It was a very hard time — some of us were just nine-years-old and we missed our parents. It was like sleepwalking. I remember some boys were lost in the bush and some others were attacked by wild animals.'

Eventually, the boys reached the Panyido refugee camp in Ethiopia — home to around 16,000 mostly boys. But things were hardly better.

'For the first month we were in the camp there was starvation and disease. Cholera took many lives,' Peter said.

He says as a nine-year-old, he was forced to grow up quickly.

'I remember we would sell what little clothing we had to get enough money to buy a doughnut. My friend and I would share the doughnut — for us, that was great day,' Peter said.

At other times a few ears of corn would be his daily food ration.

'If someone died we would just bury them in the camp. As boys, we didn't have the strength or tools to dig deep graves so sometimes the bodies would come back up if it rained and they would smell. It was a horrible time for us,' he said.

After a few months, the UNHCR arrived bringing food supplies and medicines.

'The UNHCR came and life improved. But still some people died because they got sick after eating too much food,' Peter said. 'They had not eaten much food for so long that when there was plenty of food it still made them sick. That is a horrible memory. And although things were better we still had dirty clothes, lice and scabies.'

After five years at Panyido, a change in the Ethiopian government meant that South Sudanese refuges were expelled from the country. Peter and his fellow young refugees were transferred to the giant Kakuma camp in Kenya, a home to refugees since the 1990s and still, with 60,000 residents, one of the largest camps on the planet.

'At first there were no facilities in Kakuma but the UNHCR arrived and built schools and a hospital,' Peter said. 'The camp really gave me a jump start because I went to school there.'

In Year 8 Peter won a high school scholarship that saw him attend a Kenyan government boarding school a day's travel from the camp. Sponsored by the Jesuit Refugee Service, Peter completed high school in 1999. He gained a place at university in Kenya but did not have sponsorship to take up the opportunity. Instead, the Jesuits recommended him and others to the Australian High Commission in Nairobi for resettlement. After sitting through interviews and background checks, Peter was given a visa to settle in Australia in 2003, bringing with him his two younger brothers who were also taken from their village to avoid government militia.

Peter completed a Bachelor of Commerce Degree, a Masters of Business Administration and a Masters of Finance at Victoria University between 2008 and 2015. He has since worked from humanitarian agencies — including Spectrum MRC, Red Cross and AMES Australia — helping to settle refugees in Melbourne.

'I wanted to work in the sector to give back and help people. I think it's important that people get opportunities to flourish just as I was helped when I arrived.'

He recently built a home at Melton, north-west of Melbourne, where he lives with his wife and five children.

Tragically, Peter's father was killed in the civil war and he recently lost another brother to illness. His mother still lives in South Sudan and he is in regular contact.

Another passion for Peter is working for his own community and he is especially driven to help young people. He accepts there are issues that need addressing in terms of recent negative publicity around South Sudanese youth.

'I can't deny there have been issues with some of our youth. But by far most of the kids are good kids who just want an opportunity to do something with their lives,' Peter said.

He says the issues around youth in his community are complicated and many of the young people have come here as troubled survivors of a brutal civil war.

'Many of these young people have just one parent and many of them understand the system and language here better than their parents do. This can lead to problems.

'Also in the education system here kids are placed in grades according to their age and not their capacity. Some of the older children in our community are placed in grades they are not suited to. So when they can't understand the teacher they feel pressure and eventually become disengaged. We need to motivate them to reengage and we need strong community leadership to do that.

'Refugees come with lots of skills and knowledge and can contribute to the society. After 15 years, I am Australian. I'm committed to this beautiful country and I'm thankful to the Australian government for giving me a chance to build a life. That's what some of our young people need — a chance to make something of their lives. It's all about opportunity,' Peter said.

CHAPTER 49
FINDING SAFETY AND OPPORTUNITY
— A REFUGEE'S JOURNEY

'This country gave me everything that I dreamed of as a little girl but could never have achieved in my homeland.'

This is how Kosovar-Albanian refugee Mirisha Bowler sums up the experience of fleeing her war-torn homeland and building a new life in Australia.

'Coming here was like starting a new life. It was fantastic. I could not believe the Australian Government and the people here would look after us as they did,' she said. 'They sorted out everything we needed from accommodation to health care. We were supported financially. In Kosovo I would never have dreamed this would happen. Coming to this country gave me the opportunities and the help I needed. With the support and opportunities I was given, I learned the language, I studied and started a career, I bought a house and I met a wonderful man and got married. These things could never have happened in Kosovo.'

Mirisha is sharing her story as way of acknowledging the society and the individuals who have helped her on her remarkable journey from rural idyll through war, the loss of loved ones, exile from her homeland and ultimately a new life on the other side of the world.

'When I was small I grew up in a big family. There were ten kids and we lived on a small farm,' Mirisha said. 'We had cows and a garden. They were happy times. We lived a normal life and we were an ordinary family.'

But that all changed when war came. Kosovo had been a semi-autonomous part of the old Yugoslavia, populated mostly by Albanians, and until the death of Marshall Tito in 1980, had existed harmoniously with the other constituent parts of the country. Tito's death brought a period of political instability and an economic recession leading to the rise of nationalist movements across Yugoslavia. The hard-line communists running the country after Tito sent troops to crush these movements. In Kosovo this resulted in the arrest and internment of more than half a million people. Eventually, the rise of Slobodan Milosevic and his plans for 'Greater Serbia' led to a war that claimed more than 13,500 lives and led to the displacement of 1.4 million people.

'Just as I was finishing primary school things started to get really bad. The Serbs closed our Albanian language schools and we had to study in private schools,' Mirisha said. 'The police would stop people in the street just for being Albanian and my brother was arrested and beaten up just for carrying an Albanian school text book.'

When full-scale fighting broke out in 1999, Mirisha and her family were forced to flee their idyllic farmhouse near the town of Qendresa.

'We had to leave the house and run. The Serbs were killing people and burning down houses. These weren't militia groups, this was the Serbian army and they had tanks and machine guns,' Mirisha said. 'I lost a cousin in the fighting and saw people killed in the street. I saw so much, for a long time thinking about it made me feel very emotional.'

The family was forced to move from village to village, moving secretly and often night, staying with friends and evading Serbian soldiers.

'Often we would get separated because there were ten of us and we could not contact each other because we had no mobile phones and there was very often no electricity,' Mirisha said.

After a year, the fighting ended with the intervention of NATO forces. But at first, this precipitated a mass expulsion of Kosovar Albanians as the Yugoslav forces continued to fight during the aerial bombing of Yugoslavia.

The war ended with the Kumanovo Treaty which saw Yugoslav and Serb forces agree to withdraw from Kosovo to make way for an international presence. In 2001 a UN administered Supreme Court, based in Kosovo, found that there had been 'a systematic campaign of terror, including murders, rapes, arsons and severe maltreatments'.

When Mirisha and her family returned to their home, it had been destroyed and the family lived in a farm shed for a time.

'Life was very hard for us but we were lucky in that at least we had some land that we could grow food. For many people the humanitarian airdrops of food were the only things that kept people alive,' Mirisha said. 'People were starving and everything had been destroyed.'

With life untenable for her and unable to get a job despite having teaching qualifications, Mirisha and her then by boyfriend joined the exodus to Albania.

'I had no money and had no idea what the future would hold — but I knew I couldn't stay in Kosovo. My boyfriend had an uncle in Australia and so we were able to come here as refugees,' Mirisha said.

She arrived in Australia in 2000 at the age of 23 and studied English with migrant and refugee settlement agency AMES Australia and then went to TAFE to study tourism and hospitality. She now works as a Duty Manager at the Radisson Hotel in Melbourne.

'I love my job and I love the people I work with who have supported and nurtured me,' Mirisha said. 'And I'm grateful to the Australian Government and taxpayers for giving people like me the opportunity to study and to build a new life. Australians need to know how much they have done for people like me. Because of that I want to respect this country and I want to give back. I've always felt looked after and loved in this country. The people who have helped me along the way have all told me I could do anything I wanted in this country. My teacher at AMES Jenny Monteiro, my friends Lisa and Leah especially have been especially supportive. And my husband Phillip has been my angel. He has supported me and let me be who I am,' she said.

Mirisha supports financially her parents and three siblings who remain in Kosovo; she has six siblings living in Germany.

'Australians need to know they have not just helped me but also my family in Kosovo, where people still struggle because the country has never really recovered from the war,' she said. 'We are a close family and it was that closeness that helped us survive the war.'

Mirisha recently visited Kosovo to see her parents and attend her nephew's wedding.

'It was great to see all of my family and friends. And it was wonderful to be in my homeland again. I love Kosovo but I love Australia too and this is my home now,' she said.

CHAPTER 50
REFUGEES AND MIGRANTS IN AUSTRALIA — HOW WE GOT HERE

Australia can make a legitimate claim to being the most successful multicultural society in the world. Since World War II around eight million migrants have come to Australia, including almost one million refugees. Though technically not refugees, many of the migrants who have come here in the past seventy years were fleeing poverty, post war austerity or political repression.

At 26 per cent, we have the highest proportion of people born overseas than any other high-immigration nation. And that includes New Zealand (23 per cent), Canada (22 per cent), the United States (14 per cent) and the United Kingdom (13 per cent).

Only Saudi Arabia has a higher overseas-born population; but foreigners are permitted to work there for periods but are never offered permanent residency or citizenship.

Research by the Migration Council of Australia says that migrant business owners employ more than 1.4 million people and migration is set to contribute $1.6 trillion to Australia's economy by 2050.

The Scanlon Foundation Mapping Social Cohesion survey has found that over the past decade Australia has maintained high levels of social cohesion and support for multiculturalism.

The survey's author Monash University's Professor Andrew Markus says 91 per cent of people living in Australia professed a sense of belonging to the nation with 89 per cent expressing pride in our way of life.

He said 83 per cent believed multiculturalism had been a good thing for Australia — in keeping with the results of previous surveys — and 66 per cent said Australians should do more to learn about the culture and customs of different ethnic and cultural groups in the country.

Meanwhile, 74 per cent agreed that in their local areas 'people from different nationalities or ethnic groups get on well together'.

More than one in five Australians speak a language other than English at home. The most common countries of birth after Australia were England (five per cent of the population) and New Zealand (2.5 per cent), followed by China (2.3 per cent) and India (2.1 per cent).

Since the mid-2000s, Chinese and Indian arrivals have outpaced arrivals from the UK and migration has replaced births as the driver of population growth.

So how did all this come about? Looking at all the evidence, not by accident.

The post-World War II Australian government decided the nation must 'populate or perish' and so, in 1945, The Department of Immigration was established. Since then, seven million permanent migrants have settled here.

And in 1948 — seventy years ago this year — two things happened. The Immigration Act was changed effectively allowing for the first time non-Anglo Celtic migrants to settle permanently. And Australian citizenship was created — until then Australians had been 'British subjects'.

It was not quite the end of the 'White Australia Policy' but it was a start and the beginnings of the modern, non-discriminatory immigration system we know today.

DNA evidence suggests the first people to migrate to the Australian continent most likely came from South-East Asia between 40,000 and 60,000 years ago, according to data from the old Department of Immigration.

Estimates of the Aboriginal population before European settlement range between 300,000 and 1.5 million: some 600 tribes speaking more than 200 distinct languages.

Today Aboriginal and Torres Strait Islander people account for 2.8 per cent of the country's 24 million people.

Most of the first modern migrants to Australia were unwilling arrivals: convicts from Britain sent to the penal colony of New South Wales. Until the mid-1800s, the population was dominated by British and Irish people. But the discovery of gold near Orange, NSW, in 1851 triggered a gold rush that changed the face of Australia.

Between 1851 and 1860, more than 600,000 migrants arrived: most were from the UK but around 10 per cent came from elsewhere in Europe and seven per cent from China.

Xenophobic hostility toward the newcomers focused on the Chinese, who were regarded as a threat to wages and employment, according to the Department of Immigration's history. The tension resulted in anti-Chinese riots which resulted in several deaths, leading to the colonies' first restrictions on immigration, targeting Chinese people.

The potato famine in Ireland in the late 1840s saw some 30,000 Irish migrants settle in Australia, and the push to develop Australia's outback led to a government decision to bring in 2,000 cameleers from India and Afghanistan.

Some 50,000 people, mostly men from Vanuatu and the Solomon Islands, were brought to Australia in the late 1800s to work as indentured labourers in agriculture in Queensland. They were mostly brought against their will, under the so-called 'black birding' practices, many stayed on and built a community.

At federation in 1901, three million people in the six colonies became the nation of Australia, and the new country's parliament defined it as a white man's nation.

The Immigration Restriction Act 1901 became known as the 'White Australia Policy' and was aimed at discouraging non-white migrants. It included a notorious dictation test of 50 words in a European language — immigration officials could choose any language they pleased — which applicants had to pass to migrate to Australia.

Japanese pearl divers and Malay and Filipino boat crew were exempt from the test. But there were thousands of Australians of Chinese, Syrian and Indian backgrounds who were forced to apply for documents to exempt them from the test if they travelled overseas and tried to re-enter Australia.

Immigration came to halt during WWI but in the 1920s more than 340,000 immigrants arrived — two-thirds of them assisted migrants from Britain, and small numbers of Greeks, Italians and Yugoslavs.

The Great Depression, which began in 1929, saw unemployment rates soar and public attitudes towards immigrants turn hostile. Immigration nosedived through the 1930s largely because of the depression.

In the years before WWII, as the political climate for Jews in Germany and Austria worsened, Australia agreed to accept 15,000 Jewish refugees from Europe. But just 5,000 arrived in 1939 before Jews in Europe could no longer escape.

After the war, Australia appeared to take a more generous approach, agreeing to take refugees under the international Displaced Persons Scheme and admitting more than 170,000 Europeans by 1954. More than 17,000 of them were Jews.

In 1948, parliament legislated to create Australian citizenship — before that, all Australians were British subjects. But Australia still actively sought British migrants in preference to other nationalities, with ventures like the assisted passage scheme known as the 'ten-pound pom' beginning in the late 1940s and running for almost 30 years.

However, the post-war environment saw a significant shift in Australia's attitude to migrants and set it on the path to multiculturalism. A national poll taken in 1943 found 40 per cent of Australians supported 'unlimited migration', driven in part by a critical labour shortage. The country's first-ever immigration minister Arthur Calwell promoted the idea that Australia needed to 'populate or perish'.

Australia began accepting migrants from more than 30 European countries, including the Netherlands, Austria, Belgium, Spain and West Germany. But the largest national groups of arrivals after the British were Italians and Greeks until the early 1970s.

A new family reunion policy saw some 30,000 arrivals from Eastern European nations join relatives in Australia.

More than 100,000 migrants from 30 different countries worked on the Snowy Hydro project, a hydroelectricity scheme that began in 1949 and completed in the 1970s.

The beginning of the end of the White Australia Policy came in 1958 with the abolition of the infamous dictation test. By 1960, Australia's population was ten million and around nine per cent of the population were of non-British origin, mostly Italians, Germans, Dutch, Greeks and Poles. Other restrictions on non-European migration were relaxed from 1966 and the number of arrivals started to increase accordingly.

Australia began to change rapidly. By 1971, one in three people living in Australia was a migrant or the child of a migrant.

In 1973, Labor Prime Minister Gough Whitlam changed the law to allow all migrants regardless of race or ethnicity to apply for Australian citizenship after three years of residence and his colourful immigration minister Al Grassby declared the White Australia Policy dead.

In 1975, racial discrimination was made illegal and also in the 1970s, new humanitarian or refugee intakes saw the settlement of Lebanese and Cypriot people.

This was followed by a significant wave of Indochinese arrivals displaced by the Vietnamese and Cambodian conflicts. More than 2,000 Indochinese refugees landed in boats on Australian shores in the late 1970s, but the majority of the 80,000 Indochinese permanent migrants came by air after they were formally processed by Australian officials at refugee camps in Malaysia and Thailand.

From the late 1990s, increasing numbers of asylum seekers fleeing conflict in the Middle East and Sri Lanka arrived in Australia by boat, mostly organised by people smugglers. Australia's government cracked down on what it called 'unauthorised' arrivals. Its offshore detention policy, designed to deter asylum seekers, has been criticised by the UN and human rights groups but the policy continues to have bipartisan support.

At the same time, Australia has opened the door to migrants and 'official' refugees. In each of the past few years, more than 190,000 new arrivals have settled in Australia, including between 12,000 and 18,000 refugees. Temporary arrivals including international students and those on 457 work visas were around 400,000 in 2016-17. There was also a special intake of 12,000 Syrian and Iraqi refugees announced in 2015 in response to the conflict there.

Since the 1980s, the focus of Australia's immigration policy has been on selecting migrants who fit much-needed skills criteria, along with family visas.

ABOUT AMES AUSTRALIA

AMES Australia is one of Australia's leading migrant and refugee settlement agencies. Each year it supports newly arrived migrants, refugees and asylum seekers to settle here through orientation programs, English tuition, vocational skills training and employment services.

Under its vision of 'full participation for all in a cohesive and diverse society', the organisation supports migrants and refugees to achieve their social and economic goals.

Each year AMES Australia assists more than 40,000 people to find their places in Australian society. The organisation's programs are aimed at fostering a sense of belonging among our clients and they recognise that social participation is a key ingredient in maintaining social cohesion.

AMES Australia works to create community links between its clients and the broader society.

Among the organisation's programs are the management of Melbourne's vibrant Multicultural Hub — a vital facility for the city's diverse communities — as well as social enterprises that provide training and work experience, cultural and artistic events and youth-based initiatives.

In 2017-18 AMES Australia engaged around 500 isolated or disengaged young people in positive social or educational activities and around 90 isolated refugee women were supported to set up income-producing enterprises.

Formally established in 1951, the organisation's antecedents were the hundreds of dedicated teachers who selflessly volunteered their time to help the thousands of new arrivals from post war Europe to successfully settle in Australia through the acquisition of English language skills.

Over the years the agency has continued to grow in numbers and expand its services.

AMES Australia has been at the forefront of significant social change, supporting new arrivals as they begin to contribute economically and socially to our diverse communities.

The organisation was intrinsic in implementing the notion of multiculturalism; a term that was new in the 1970s but which now is accepted as an accurate description of the cultural and ethnic diversity of contemporary Australia.

AMES
Australia

Contact AMES: 132637
Website: www.ames.net.au
Services: www.ames.net.au/settle-in-aus
Volunteering:
www.ames.net.au/volunteering/why-volunteer-with-ames-australia

Any profits from the sale of this book will go towards supporting refugees and asylum seekers in need.

ACKNOWLEDGEMENTS

A lot of people have contributed to this book.

First and foremost, I'd like to thank the refugees who were brave enough to share their stories with us. You are all inspirational people from whom we have learnt the true meanings of courage, humility and resilience.

In different ways Cesira Colleluori, Diane Zammitt, Helen Matovu-Reed, Sheree Petersen, Peter Kelly, Jess Duncan, Jess Philips, Linh Ly, Barat Ali Batoor, Abdul Ibrahim, Adam Baxter, Sarah Gilmore, Carissa Gilham, James Brincat, John and Marg Millington, Annmarie Power, Gabrielle Chen, Vivian Jiang, Norma Medawar, Ruby Brown, Diane Tabbagh, Nanthu Kunoo, Obaidullah Mehak, Susy Barry, Melika Sheikh-Eldin, Tom Danks and Portia Conyers-East have all played a part in the realisation of this project.

I'd also like to thank Jess and Michael at Wilkinson Publishing and my boss Cath Scarth for her leadership and guidance.

Thanks also to my family Leanne and Sam for putting up with me.